# BEST GHOST TALES
## OF NORTH CAROLINA

### Second Edition

# $\mathscr{B}$EST GHOST TALES

# OF NORTH CAROLINA

## Second Edition

## Terrance Zepke

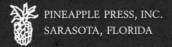

PINEAPPLE PRESS, INC.
SARASOTA, FLORIDA

To all the members of the
Carolina Ghost Watch Club

*Thanks for your supernatural knowledge, your boundless
enthusiasm, and for keeping our ghosts alive!*

Inquiries should be addressed to:

Pineapple Press, Inc.
P.O. Box 3889
Sarasota, Florida 34230
www.pineapplepress.com

Library of Congress Cataloging-in-Publication Data

Zepke, Terrance
  Best ghost tales of North Carolina / Terrance Zepke.-- 2nd ed.
      p. cm.
  Rev. ed. of: The best ghost tales of North Carolina.
  Includes index.
  ISBN-13: 978-1-56164-378-3 (pbk. : alk. paper)
  ISBN-10: 1-56164-378-5 (pbk. : alk. paper)
  1.  Ghosts--North Carolina. 2.  Haunted houses--North Carolina.  I. Zepke,
Terrance, Best ghost tales of North Carolina. II. Title.
  BF1472.U6Z45 2006
  133.109756--dc22
                                    2006002744

Second Edition
10 9 8 7 6 5 4 3 2

Printed in the United States of America

*When the footpads quail at the night-bird's wail,*
*And black dogs bay at the moon,*
*Then is the specter's holiday—then is the ghosts' high noon!*
Sir William Schwenck Gilbert (1887)

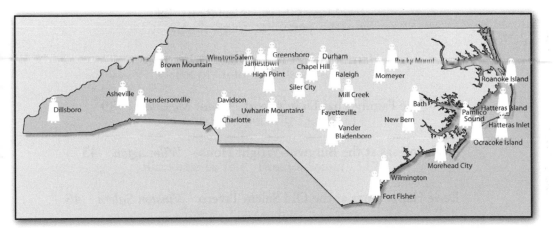

# INTRODUCTION

*W*hat are ghosts? Guardian angels? Lingering spirits of loved ones? Balls of energy that manifest themselves in various forms? Or are they a trick of the mind, as some would have us believe?

Ever since I can remember, I have loved reading and listening to ghost stories. They are so intriguing on the surface, I guess I never wanted to examine the issue too closely, just in case I stumbled across scientific justification of the origin of the Brown Mountain Lights or what actually happened to the mystery ship, *Carroll A. Deering*.

When I wrote *Ghosts of the Carolina Coasts*, I did not probe into the subject of ghosts from an academic standpoint. I concentrated on relaying some wonderful stories that took place from North Carolina's Outer Banks to the Low Country of South Carolina. I was certain I would end up writing another book on the subject, focused exclusively on North Carolina's folklore.

When the publisher asked if I'd be interested in working on a second edition of *The Best Ghost Tales of North Carolina*, I jumped at the chance. A second edition is an opportunity to make significant revisions. Just what does this mean for you, reader? First and foremost, I have added new tidbits of information I have been able to find about the original stories. This includes better directions to haunted sites, witnesses I didn't know about previously, and even more extensive research. I also sneaked in a few new stories—more ghosts! Finally, I got to update and expand the "How to Conduct Your Own Ghost Hunt" chapter.

Determining which stories are "the *best* ghost tales of North Carolina" was of course difficult and, finally, arbitrary. I knew I had to include some well-known stories, but I wanted to share some lesser-known tales. In addition, the end result needed to be a good representation of ghosts across the state—not just my favorites or the more popular specters.

When I started working on this book, I decided it was high time to address the ghost issue. Do ghosts really exist? If so, who or what are they? I discovered that this is a very complicated matter. Some

# Legend of the Gimghoul Castle

Chapel Hill

*The Order of the Gimghouls have placed floodlights that illumi-*
*nate the castle and grounds at night and have posted several "No*
*Trespassing" signs to let curiosity seekers know that they are not*
*wanted—or tolerated.*

*P*eter Dromgoole came to the University of
North Carolina at Chapel Hill in 1831, but the eighteen-year-old
failed his admissions test. After an argument with the professor
who administered the test, the irate young man almost left Chapel Hill in a fit of temper. The spoiled lad really wasn't interested
in school, but he didn't want to go home and tell everyone he
hadn't been accepted at Carolina. Dromgoole stayed and hired a
tutor, presumably to help him pass the entrance exam at a later
date.

However, scholastics took a backseat to Dromgoole's real
passions: playing cards and chasing women. Legend has it that
the playboy met his match when he encountered a young woman
named Fanny. The two usually met at Piney Prospect, which is
the highest point in Chapel Hill. Peter and Fanny had an arrange-
ment that suited them, and the pair carried on until a jealous rival
created trouble. Another man became obsessed with Fanny and
challenged Dromgoole to a pistol duel. Male pride forced Peter to
accept even though his competitor's skills were superior.

Late one night, the two men squared off at Piney Prospect.
An old slave noticed the men getting ready to duel and ran to tell
Miss Fanny. The frightened woman ran as fast as she could but
Dromgoole had already been shot by the time she arrived. Sobbing uncontrollably, she had no choice but to cradle her lover in
her arms as he died. Witnesses to the deadly confrontation did
not want their participation revealed, and they agreed to keep secret what had transpired that night. The men quickly dug a shallow grave, put the body in it, and covered it with a large stone.

This big rock later became known as Dromgoole's Tomb.

For a while, Fanny continued to go to Piney Prospect every day, where she felt closer to Peter. She would sit in front of the rock under which he was buried, alternately weeping, talking to him, and lovingly touching the slab that served as his tombstone. The heartbroken woman died shortly after Peter Dromgoole. Many believe that the site of this tragedy, including the castle that was later built near Dromgoole's Tomb, is haunted. Legend has it that sobbing and wailing are still heard at times. The large stone that is known as Dromgoole's Tomb is stained red, and whenever it rains a liquid that looks like blood seeps out of it.

According to James Vickers' *Chapel Hill: An Illustrated History* (Barclay, 1985), Peter's uncle heard the story of the duel and traveled to Chapel Hill to investigate. However, Congressman George Dromgoole was unable to find evidence of foul play or discover the truth about his nephew's abrupt and mysterious disappearance. A letter written by Peter Dromgoole's roommate, John Buxton Williams, attempted to dispel speculation. In his letter, the man denied there had been any violent encounter. Williams stated that Dromgoole "had simply left on a public stage." Some dismissed this, believing that the affluent Virginian family had pressured Dromgoole's roommate to write the letter to save the family's reputation from scandal.

Bruce Cotton, a descendant of Peter Dromgoole, found three letters from Peter Dromgoole to his family at the Brunswick County, Virginia, homestead, and published them in the November 1924 issue of *Carolina* (the campus magazine). These letters support the story that Dromgoole failed his admissions test and then hired a tutor. In April 1833, the youth wrote his last letter, disclosing he was depressed and telling his father he was going to Europe. After this communication, he was never heard from again. Cotton believes Dromgoole did not go to Europe. Instead, he thinks the young man joined the army using his former roommate's name and then moved to Texas, where he died in a gunfight.

Dr. Kemp Plummer Battle, a former president of the University of North Carolina at Chapel Hill, wrote *History of the University of North Carolina*. In this publication Battle mentions the Dromgoole legend. He is of the belief that Peter Dromgoole left UNC–Chapel Hill and migrated to the Southwest, where he was subsequently killed in a bar fight, possibly over a woman or a card game.

Chapel Hill has two historic districts: the UNC–Chapel Hill campus and the Gimghoul District, where Piney Prospect and the magnificent castle are located. Originally called Hippol Castle, the building has been dubbed Dromgoole's Castle because of the legendary duel. It is also popularly known as Gimghoul Castle because it has been the gothic meeting place for the Order of the Gimghouls for many decades. Not much is known about the castle or the secret society that owns it.

The idea of building such a structure on this site originally belonged to Edwin Wray Martin, a former University of North Carolina student. The strange young man liked to climb up to Piney Prospect and roam the dense forest, envisioning a magical wonderland filled with warlocks and goblins. He dubbed the woods "Glandon Forest" and dreamed of an imposing, medieval edifice in the midst of the forest where he and other like-minded men could meet. Edwin Martin founded a small fraternity in 1889 based on his beliefs and ideals. The Order of the Gimghouls started out with just five members, including Martin. Before realizing his dream, Martin died in 1895, but the fraternity lived on. Members made shrewd and aggressive land deals, starting with the purchase of ninety-five acres. Subsequently, they traded part of that land to the university, sold some acres, and developed forty acres into a neighborhood. Using money earned from these deals, the society built the fabulous Gimghoul Castle.

The $50,000 construction project began in the early 1920s and took more than four years to complete. The massive gothic structure required 1,300 tons of well-rounded stones. A crew of French stonecutters did the work. The workmen were brought from Valdese and spoke no English. Not only were they the best stonecutters, but because they spoke no English, they couldn't reveal information about

**Inside the castle...**

Although we don't know much about the décor of the castle, we do know that it has housed many unique and expensive antiques and artwork. Some have been removed or stolen over the years, but many exceptional items remain inside the castle. A large painting done by Charles Baskerville Jr. hangs on a castle wall. Baskerville (April 16, 1896–November 20, 1994) remains a renowned artist whose work is widely respected. One of his many admirers was Jacqueline Kennedy Onassis, who owned two of his works: a watercolor-and-pencil sketch, "Tiger," and a painting, "Guardians of the Portal of the Temple." They fetched $40,250 and $23,000, respectively, in her estate auction in 1996. Baskerville donated the valuable painting "George and the Dragon" to the secret Gimghoul society shortly after the castle was built, in honor of his father, who had been a member.

the castle to outsiders. The Order of the Gimghouls is very protective of their secrets. Very few non-members have ever been allowed inside the castle, but those who have managed to gain access say it is spectacular. They report there is a large banquet room, tower room, kitchen, caretaker's apartment, and grand spiral staircase. Once upon a time, there was medieval armor in the banquet room, but it was stolen many years ago.

The Order of the Gimghouls have placed floodlights to illuminate the castle and grounds at night and have posted several "No Trespassing" signs to let curiosity seekers know that they are not wanted—or tolerated. There is a live-in caretaker and police are dispatched when intrusions take place. The society allegedly consists of notable alumni (including prominent businessmen and well-known politicians), as well as some students and professors. Membership is usually "by legacy" and men are inducted periodically in elaborate ceremonies.

The secret fraternity published a booklet about the Gimghoul legend in 1978. The legend describes a figure in a heavy, dark, hooded robe who appears at Dromgoole's room in South Building and uses an extended arm to signal Peter Dromgoole to the hilltop. This sinister figure is supposedly the unknown assailant who killed Dromgoole during the pistol duel. The booklet also claims that the ghost of Dromgoole rises from his grave at midnight on the anniversary of his death. The secret society also divulged its emblem and its symbolism in this booklet. It is a ghoul behind a broken pillar holding a cross in his left hand and a key in his right. The key opens the Dark Secret of the Gimghouls and the cross represents the Dark Secret—whatever it is.

*If you're going . . .*
The castle is east of the University of North Carolina at Chapel Hill campus. Take Highway 54 West into Chapel Hill. Turn right at the first stop light at the top of the hill. Take the next right onto Gimghoul Road. Follow it until it ends, about a mile or so. You'll see a private dirt road to the castle. You'll also see the castle through the trees. Parking will be a problem as there is limited street parking available. University of North Carolina at Chapel Hill was the state's first university, founded in 1795.

# MYSTERY OF THE BROWN MOUNTAIN LIGHTS

Linville

*Through the years, many scientific theories have been presented, although they are as flawed as those theories that preceded them.*

*D*espite sightings by hundreds of residents and visitors alike over the years, as well as numerous official and unofficial investigations, the Brown Mountain Lights will remain one of life's little mysteries, as well as the state's biggest and best-known legend.

In the foothills of the Blue Ridge Mountains, this small, 2,600-foot elevation in Burke County would rarely be discussed or visited if it weren't home to the mysterious lights. Just what the lights look like is as big a source of dispute as their origin. Some see a small reddish light that rises over the summit and then disappears shortly thereafter. It appears again within minutes but at another area of the mountain. It rises, hovers, and disappears. The pattern repeats itself throughout the night. Other witnesses claim the light is definitely white and moves in a circular fashion—appearing and disappearing in the same area. Still others seem certain the light is like a glowing ball of yellowish fire.

I spoke to a young man from Thomasville who claimed to have seen the light and said it was a bright, round, yellowish-red light. As it got higher, it got smaller and then disappeared. A minute or two later the same round, bright, yellowish-red light appeared elsewhere over the mountain. It disappeared and appeared again further over on the mountain. This occurred several times.

My mother is another witness to the famed Brown Mountain Lights. She told me that her father once took the family to the mountains and they saw the notorious lights. She was very young at the time, around ten or eleven years old, and can't recall much about them. She thinks there were more than one and that the lights "flicked on and off" several times. Whether the light is white, red, or yellow—stationary or in motion—all witnesses agree they could not determine the origin of the light.

These are alternate terms for swamp gas, which is a natural phenomenon caused by decaying organic matter in bogs and other swampy areas. Certain fungi on rotting wood transforms into a gaseous state and, on rare occasions, takes on an eerie glow or luminescence. Swamp gas is a popular theory scientific experts use to explain strange lights and activities that have been seen by many witnesses over the years. *This theory is hard to believe since there are no bogs or marshes in area. Foxfire light is not constant or bright enough for this theory to be true.*

- Reflections from nearby towns, such as Hickory and Lenoir. *The lights were seen long before the advent of electricity.*

- Andes Lights (a phenomenon that occurs in South America's Andes Mountains when electricity discharges pass through the clouds to the mountaintops, thereby emitting a light). Dr. W.J. Humphries of the U.S. Weather Bureau suggested this theory. *But this can only occur at extremely high altitudes, which would disqualify Brown Mountain.*

- St. Elmo's Fire (an electrical discharge that occurs in conjunction with a thunderstorm in certain atmospheric conditions). *The Smithsonian Institutition dismissed this theory because it wouldn't occur mid-air as the Brown Mountain Lights do, and the lights appear without an accompanying storm.*

- Desert mirage (putting it simply, air currents of different and unequal densities could possibly produce reflecting surfaces from which really bright stars could be reflected). *This theory is remotely possible.*

The scientific community is no longer concerned with the mystery of the Brown Mountain Lights, probably because they are unable to find a satisfactory scientific conclusion. Perhaps they have finally accepted it as a natural phenomenon or unsolved mystery.

*If you're going . . .*
There is even controversy over the best place to see the lights.
- Some recommend Brown Mountain Overlook. Take NC 181 to

(A sign posted at one of the viewing areas).

**BROWN MOUNTAIN LIGHTS. THE LONG, EVEN-CRESTED MTN. IN THE DISTANCE IS BROWN MTN. FROM EARLY TIMES PEOPLE HAVE OBSERVED WEIRD, WAVERING LIGHTS RISE ABOVE THIS MTN. THEN DWINDLE AND FADE AWAY**

Mile Marker #20, which is twenty miles northwest of Morganton and one mile south of the Barkhouse Picnic Area.

- Others claim Lost Cove Cliffs Overlook is the spot. Take the Blue Ridge Parkway to milepost 310, about two miles north of the NC 181 junction. Grandfather Mountain and Blowing Rock are also good spots
- Most agree the best place is Wiseman's View Overlook. Take Kistler Memorial Highway (also called NC 105 or State Road 1238) five miles south of the village at Linville Falls.

The best chance of seeing the lights is in the fall on a cool, clear night, and the best time of night is at 8 or 9, possibly even 10 P.M. Even if you don't see the lights, you're guaranteed a pretty view of the gorge. While you're in the area, you may want to check out Mount Mitchell. At 6,684 feet of elevation, this is the highest mountain in the eastern U.S. Other nearby points of interest include Grandfather Mountain, with its mile-high swinging bridge, and Linville Caverns and Falls. Brown Mountain is part of Pisgah National Forest. For more information, see www.recreation.gov

# *L*YDIA, THE VANISHING LADY

Jamestown

*Ever since that tragic night in 1923, a young lady garbed in a white ball gown has often been spotted on the side of the road waving for help.*

This must be the most widely circulated story in the state. Many hitchhiking ghost tales I've heard are nothing more than variations of this story. The original story is about a girl named Lydia who had been at a dance in Raleigh with her boyfriend. In the early 1900s, a road was paved that linked Greensboro to High Point. The road ran through Jamestown and a narrow underpass beneath the railroad tracks. The pair was probably discussing what a wonderful evening it had been, perhaps even making future plans, as they drove home to High Point. It was a dark night and the drivers were not paying as much attention as they should. Lydia and her boyfriend collided with another car at the underpass, and Lydia was killed instantly. Ever since that tragic night in 1923, a young lady garbed in a white ball gown has often been spotted on the side of the road waving for help.

Burke Hardison is one of the motorists who have seen the specter. It was very late as he passed through Jamestown. As Hardison approached the underpass, he saw a girl wearing a light-colored dress. She was frantically signaling for help. Knowing something must be terribly wrong for this lovely young woman to be all dressed up and standing alone on the side of the road at that time of night, he quickly pulled over.

"What's the matter?" Hardison asked with concern. The girl told him that she was desperately trying to get home to High Point. "My mother will be terribly worried," she said softly. He told her to get in and he would gladly take her home. She said, "Thank you," and gave him the address as she got in the vehicle. Lydia leaned wearily back in the seat and offered no more information as she closed her eyes. Although he was dying of curiosity, Hardison didn't ask her any questions.

He knew how to get to the street she had named so he turned

off the highway and continued without saying a word. He glanced over at his passenger and noticed she looked as if she was sleeping. Hardison wondered how long she had been waiting for someone to come by. What was her story? He thought he might find out when they reached their destination, but when he went around to open her door, she was gone. It wasn't possible, but she had vanished!

Determined to get to the bottom of the bizarre occurrence, Hardison marched up to the door and knocked. After a few minutes, a woman answered. Before the odd tale could be told, the sad-looking woman said, "I know why you're here. You think you picked up my daughter. You're not the first person this has happened to, and you almost assuredly won't be the last." She explained how her daughter had been killed in a car wreck some years ago. The woman told him that motorists occasionally showed up claiming they had given a girl a ride home but she had disappeared upon arriving at the house.

She seems so tired and troubled that no one ever presses the girl for more information. The few times those who picked her up tried, all they got out of her was that her name was Lydia and that she wanted to get home as soon as possible. With tears welling up in her eyes, the woman told Hardison that she wished someone could bring her daughter home.

I interviewed a Jamestown resident who thinks he saw Lydia when he was a teenager. He asked that I not print his name but admitted that he saw what he believes was Lydia. Years ago, there was a dirt road that extended to the area around the underpass. He was out one rainy night with some other youths on that road when his truck got stuck in the mud. The boys got out to push the vehicle and he saw something white behind him. They didn't stick around to get a better look. They ran off and didn't come back for the car until the next day. I talked to several other longtime residents of Jamestown, but no one knows just when Lydia was last seen. I was told the best chance of seeing her is on foggy or rainy nights.

Pranks have occurred due to the folklore surrounding Lydia. High school students have outfitted themselves in fancy white dresses and appeared as cars approached the underpass. But those who say they have picked up Lydia on the side of the road say it is no laughing matter. They are haunted by the image of a beautiful young woman trying to get home but never quite making it.

*If you're going . . .*

The old underpass (also known as Lydia's Bridge) was located on Highway 70 (now High Point Road). It you're coming from Greensboro, follow High Point Road and look for the "Welcome to Jamestown" sign. The sign is near the new overpass, which is about 40 or 50 feet east of Lydia's Bridge. The old bridge can barely be seen from the road due to all the overgrowth. To get a good view, you'll have to park up the road and walk back, being careful of traffic. Be sure to wear something appropriate for walking through thick vegetation.

*This is the original underpass where Lydia was killed. It is located about a hundred feet from the underpass now in use.*

# Too Many Ghosts

## New Bern

*Most disturbing of all were the sightings. Men were seen in different rooms of the house for a moment or two before they vanished.*

$I$n the early 1800s, Captain Edward B. Tinker carried out a most evil plan. Captain Tinker was returning to New Bern from Baltimore, where he picked up some valuable cargo. An awful storm arrived as the captain and his men were crossing the Pamlico Sound. The crew had a devil of a time keeping the ship afloat. During the ordeal, Captain Tinker had some of the heavy cargo loaded onto the lifeboats. This was standard practice, to help keep the ship from sinking.

It seems the storm was the perfect opportunity for the greedy captain. When the fierce weather subsided and the cargo was unloaded back onto the ship, it was discovered that some of it was missing. Coincidentally, what had vanished was a significant amount of gold! The captain dismissed the problem by saying that it had probably been lost at sea during the hasty transfer. He asked the crew to sign sworn statements corroborating his account. All agreed, except a cabin boy named Edward. The lad suspected the captain had stolen the gold for himself and his accomplices, although he was too smart to flat out accuse their leader.

Captain Tinker did not seem to have a problem with the boy's lack of cooperation. In fact, he asked Edward to join his crew for the journey from New Bern to the captain's plantation on Brice's Creek. The trip was nearly over when Tinker announced that he felt like going duck hunting. It would be the perfect welcome-home meal, he said.

"Go roust the fowl! I can already taste my supper!" he growled. He pointed out a favorite resting place for the area waterfowl. "Just over on the other side of that marsh," he told the youth as he pointed out the spot. When the birds flew out of the marsh, Captain Tinker would shoot them. Enough supper for everyone, he promised. The boy was pleased to hear that since there hadn't been much meat on the journey. He was tired of stew and hard tack. But when the boy shooed the birds out into the clearing, Tinker took careful aim and shot the boy instead of the birds! He tied rocks to the boy's body to weigh it down and then dumped it into the river.

That would take care of any loose lips regarding the missing cargo, he thought. The callous captain was sure his crime would never be revealed. After all, there were no witnesses except a couple members of his crew. He was certain they wouldn't talk. Unfortunately for him, the rocks used to weigh down the slim body came loose, allowing the corpse to float to shore. It wasn't long before the body was found. Captain Tinker was arrested for the boy's murder soon thereafter. However, before he could be brought to trial, the savvy seaman bribed a guard and escaped to Philadelphia.

Fortunately, he was soon apprehended and brought back to New Bern to stand trial for murder. One of the trusted crew members aboard ship at the time that Tinker shot Edward testified that he had seen their captain shoot that boy. He was loyal, he swore, but witnessing the murder of that innocent boy was just too much for his conscience. Killing a man when your back's to the wall is one thing, but taking the life of a defenseless boy was just inexcusable, he told the court. Captain Tinker was found guilty and hanged in 1811.

Until his execution, Tinker resided in a house (circa early 1800s) on Craven Street, known as the Hannah Clark House. From the time of his death until the structure was demolished in 1935, it was reportedly haunted. Residents swore they heard voices in empty rooms. When it was razed, workmen found a skeleton buried in a shallow grave under the house. Despite much speculation, its identity was never discovered.

The John Wright Stanly House was eventually moved from its original location to the site of the former Hannah Clark House. It was reportedly haunted even before it was relocated. The cook was shot by her ex-husband, who then turned the gun on himself. The bodies were found side by side on the kitchen floor. Some months later, the lady of the house, Mrs. Farrow, and her mother, Mrs. Morris, were in the kitchen discussing the matter.

As they talked, they glanced at the rocking chair in the corner of the kitchen, remembering how their former cook had loved sitting in it. The chair began moving as if someone were in it. With a swift consistent motion, the chair rocked back and forth. As the women watched, the chair stopped rocking just as quickly as it had begun, and the room suddenly felt very cold. Mrs. Farrow also reported hearing water running in the kitchen sink on two or three occasions. When she checked it, the faucet was always turned off but there was water in the sink. The sound of feet padding across the room was also heard, but when someone checked to see if anyone was in the kitchen, no one was discovered. Could it be the cook reminding them that it was still her kitchen?

Most disturbing of all were the sightings. Men have been seen in various rooms of the house for about a minute before they vanish. Neighbors reported ghost sightings and sounds at night. Many believe these male specters are descendants of Governor Richard Dobbs Spaight Sr., who lived in the John Wright Stanly House. In 1802, Congressman John Stanly, son of John Wright Stanly, killed Spaight in a political duel in New Bern.

Some believe the strange activities and sightings may be Captain Tinker, who refuses to leave his old homesite. Still others believe that the spirit of the corpse that was found when the Hannah Clark House was demolished may haunt the property.

So who haunts this house? Is it the cook who was killed by her ex-husband? Is it the man who killed his ex-wife (the cook) and then killed himself? Is it a member of the Spaight family? Or is it a member of the Stanly family? Could it be Captain Tinker? Or the youth who was murdered by Captain Tinker? What about the spirit of the corpse found in a grave under the Hannah Clark House? We'll probably never know the answer, but it's a safe bet that more than one restless spirit roams this old house.

*If you're going . . .*
The John Wright Stanly House (1783) is one of New Bern's best examples of Georgian architecture. The mansion also houses an im-

pressive collection of period antiques and collectibles. Stanley was a devoted patriot during the American Revolution. President George Washington spent several days in this fine home during a southern campaign. The house is open to the public for tours. For more information, contact the Craven County Visitor's Information Center at (800) 437-5767 or visit www.visitnewbern.com

### Haunted Places . . .

While the Carolinas boast numerous haunted sites, the supernatural can be found just about everywhere. Some of America's most famous haunted places include Gettysburg (Pennsylvania), the Alamo (Texas), Hotel Del Coronado (California), Equinox (Vermont), and the White House (Washington, D.C.). The White House is reportedly haunted by former President Abraham Lincoln. It's generally believed that his ghost appears whenever America is in serious turmoil or crisis. While her husband was president, Eleanor Roosevelt allegedly communicated with Lincoln through séances. Some maids reported seeing a ghost during Harry Truman's administration. Rosalyn Carter refused to discuss it, and Jacqueline Kennedy told the media that she "took great comfort in it."

# HERMIT OF FORT FISHER

## Fort Fisher

*For seventeen years he lived in an old World War II bunker and was pretty much self-sufficient, living on berries, fish, shrimp, oysters, and vegetables that he grew.*

Robert Edward Harrell was born on February 2, 1893, and he was put into a county rest home in Shelby, North Carolina, in 1955. That might have been the end of the story, but it is just the beginning of this tale. Determined that he was not going to be confined, Harrell ran away to Fort Fisher, where he lived until his death on June 4, 1972. Before retreating from society, Harrell had many jobs, including being a printer, a street vendor selling trinkets and jewelry, a machinist, a farm worker, and a coal miner. Five years after he left the care facility and made his home at Fort Fisher, his family finally learned of his whereabouts. I'm sure they tried to convince him to abandon his new life, but were unsuccessful in their endeavors.

For seventeen years he lived in an old World War II bunker and was pretty much self-sufficient, living on berries, fish, shrimp, oysters, and vegetables that he grew. During the winter and other lean times, the Hermit relied on the kindness of others for food. Harrell made periodic trips into town to get provisions he was unable to grow or catch himself. He revealed these insights into his life during a rare interview with a staff member of the Center for Southern Folklore.

---

**Another disturbing element in this unsolved mystery . . .**

I found a videotaped interview between the Hermit and a staff member of the Center for Southern Folklore in a public library. After watching the documentary, I contacted the center to obtain more information. But no one at the center knew what I was talking about! Judy Peizer, who has been the center's director for many years, told me that the center had never participated in the interview or video. She said the center exists for the preservation of oral storytelling and performance art and that none of its employees would have been involved in such a project, even on a freelance basis. She was completely baffled when asked why the center was credited with the project. Since the interviewer remained off camera and only the Hermit was recorded, there is no way of knowing who was responsible for making the video.

---

The recluse informed the interviewer that he did not eat many square meals, as he was just too busy. Harrell told family and visitors to Fort Fisher that he had moved there to write a book. He claims he finished a four-hundred-page manuscript, *A Tyrant in Every House*, and sent it to his sister in Charlotte for safekeeping. The Hermit also told the interviewer that he had a son and nine grandchildren in Cleveland, Ohio. He said his son came to visit once a year, until his son's death.

The colorful coot said he loved people, especially the underdog, the handicapped, and the working man. Indeed, he was friendly to everyone who spoke to him. As word spread about the Hermit of Fort Fisher, he became something of a tourist attraction. Although he made his home in the bunker, which was closed off by loose two-by-fours placed haphazardly around the entrance, Harrell claimed he spent most nights outside in the marsh.

Yet the Hermit was found dead *inside* the bunker with the two-by-fours barricading the entrance. The body was lying spread-eagle and a raincoat was bunched around his neck. These facts seem very suspicious. First, Harrell slept outside most nights. Second, spread-eagle is not a natural sleeping position. Third, even if he had been wearing the raincoat for warmth, he wouldn't wear it bunched up around his neck. Furthermore, it would be nearly impossible to manage to get a coat into such a position while sleeping.

Shoe prints were found in the sand that could have belonged to someone who dragged Harrell's body back to the bunker. Authorities who investigated his death believed he had a heart attack but managed to crawl from the marsh back inside the bunker. But that would mean that Harrell not only made it all the way into the bunker from the marsh but was also able to put the two-by-fours in front of the bunker entrance before finally dying?

It doesn't seem plausible. Long-time acquaintances, such as Gail Welker, are not swallowing this far-fetched story. Since there was evidence of a struggle, she is of the opinion that he was killed for the money he kept on hand to buy supplies. Supposedly, the Hermit hid his money in old jars and buried them in the sand. For whatever reason, officials did not pursue this possibility. During the interview conducted by the Center for Southern Folklore, the Hermit said he had been threatened, even beaten, while living on Fort Fisher.

So what did happen? Did local hoodlums accidentally beat up the old man so badly they killed him and then tried to conceal it? Did they cause him to have a heart attack and then leave him for dead? Did robbers murder him for his buried money? Did developers who wanted the squatter off the prime piece of real estate murder him? Did he die a natural death? Some say we'll never know because the State Bureau of Investigation and the local sheriff's department bungled the investigation. Critics say the body should have been autopsied before it was buried. They claim a sloppy and half-hearted investigation was conducted and that those involved tried to conceal that fact.

What we do know is that Captain H.G. Grohman, chief of detectives with the sheriff's department, got a call from the Carolina Beach Police informing him that the Hermit was dead. Grohman called Fred Pickler, the department's unofficial photographer, to come with him and take the crime scene photographs. When the men arrived they found a track extended thirty feet from the bunker doorway to the edge of the marsh. The captain thought it looked like the Hermit had suffered a heart attack, crawled back inside the bunker, and died. Pickler said it looked like someone had dragged the body by the feet, which would explain why the coat was bunched up around the neck. He photographed the body, the mysterious tracks, and tire marks from a four-wheel-drive vehicle, which appeared to be fresh. One of the photos clearly shows that two-by-fours were in front of the bunker entrance, which makes it impossible to believe that the old man put them up while he was having a heart attack. A plaster of the tire tracks was also made.

If the Hermit was murdered for his money, then why didn't the robbers steal the money? We don't know how much money Harrell had to start with, but deputies found $300 hidden in cans and jars. Did they take what they could readily find? Did they get scared and flee before finding all the money? Or was robbery never the motive?

The body was taken to the morgue at New Hanover Memorial Hospital. Without performing an autopsy, the medical examiner determined the cause of death to be "heart attack." How he made this determination without a proper post-mortem examination is curious. Curtis Register, the SBI special agent sent to investigate the death, reviewed the evidence and came to the conclusion that the questionable tracks were made by a body that was dragged. But the agent didn't feel he had enough evidence to officially call it a murder. The case was closed six months later for lack of evidence.

Beth Purvis Farmer revealed that when she was a teenager, she and a couple of her friends used to check on the old man sometimes. One time he told them he had been harassed. The Hermit even named the culprits. She claims to have made a statement to that effect to the local authorities after the Hermit's death, but Sheriff Grohman doesn't recall any such statement. Rumors of five rough locals harassing the Hermit on the night of his death remain unproven.

Some time after the mysterious video about the Hermit was produced, authorities reopened the investigation into the death of Robert Edward Harrell. The SBI questioned a suspect but didn't have any proof against him, so no one was charged. The body was sent to Chapel Hill, where the state's chief coroner performed the autopsy. The medical examiner said the body was so badly decomposed that it was hard to discover the truth at this point in time. He seconded the earlier conclusion of "natural death."

The Hermit Society was founded in 1993 by fans of the Hermit to uncover the truth. Unfortunately, they were unable to put the mystery to rest. Did something sinister happen to the Hermit that night, or is it all much ado about an old man who suffered a heart attack? We'll probably never know since the police captain and the forensic photographer do not agree on what they saw at the crime scene. Of particular interest is that neither the coroner nor the chief deputy on the original case can be questioned since both committed suicide. In addition, there are no notes to review since the investigation file, including key evidence, has disappeared. Furthermore, crime scene photographer Fred Pickler will no longer discuss the case.

The good news is that the land was never developed. It has become the Fort Fisher State Recreation Site. A Fort Fisher Hermit Marker reminds visitors that Robert Edward Harrell once called the land home. In 1989, the Hermit's remains were moved from a cemetery in Shelby, North Carolina, back to the Fort Fisher area. He was reburied in the Federal Point Methodist Church Cemetery. It is said that on the anniversary of his death, voices have been heard in the area where Harrell once lived. Visitors to Fort Fisher can follow Hermit Trail, which leads to his beloved marshland. Listen carefully. Does the Hermit of Fort Fisher haunt his old homesite?

Or is it haunted by another spirit? During the Civil War, Fort Fisher was vital in keeping the Wilmington port open for Confederate supplies and commissions. The fortification was comprised mainly of dirt and sand, used to withstand explosives. The Federals were certain they could win the war if they could secure Fort Fisher. On December 7, 1864, Union soldiers fired on the stronghold for twenty days but were deterred by Confederate troops. The Federal troops began their second assault on Fort Fisher on January 13, 1865. The Confederates put up a brave counterattack but were forced to surrender two days later. Two thousand men died defending Fort Fisher. Unaccounted-for footsteps have been heard and a ghostly apparition of a Confederate officer has been seen looking over the rampart toward the sea. Some believe it is the ghost of General William Whiting, a fort commander who was wounded during battle and who later died in a prison camp.

*If you're going . . .*

Fort Fisher Historic Site is the third-most visited historical site in the state. It is located off Highway 421, near Kure Beach. Ten percent of Fort Fisher is intact. The land and sea attack against Fort Fisher during January 1865 was the largest waterborne assault on a mainland target until the allied invasion of Normandy during WWII.

The newly renovated Fort Fisher Civil War Museum can be found nearby, as well as the Fort Fisher State Recreation Site. The state park is at the southern tip of the island and includes more than four miles of pristine beach and marsh. The Fort Fisher Ferry landing is just south of the Fort Fisher Historic Site. Ferry reservations are highly suggested (800-BY-FERRY). For more information, call (910) 458-5538/5798 or visit www.ah.dcr.state.nc.us/sections/hs/fisher/fisher.htm.

# THE FAMILY THAT DIDN'T EXIST

Cedar Mountain

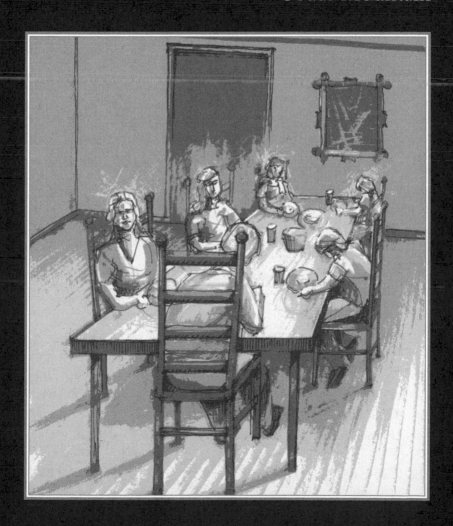

*He was seen on occasion by passersby, chopping wood and tending to other daily responsibilities, but he never left the area around his cabin. He became a recluse.*

The Uwharrie Mountains are located in central North Carolina, overlooking the Yadkin River. Until the mid-1700s, Indians and wildlife were the only inhabitants, but white settlers began arriving in great numbers. Since that time, the area has seen many changes. Battles have been fought over the land, including some between the Indians and settlers. Moonshiners have made their home in these mountains because the hillsides and valleys make good hiding spots from the law. Most of the residents are descendants of "mountain folk" and wouldn't live anywhere else on earth.

The Reeves family was a fine example of simple mountain people. They loved their home, which was situated at the base of Cedar Mountain, a wee part of the Uwharries. The family of six, including the parents, Jubal and Rebekah, lived in a small, but cozy cabin. They didn't have much money, but their basic needs were met and the home was filled with love and warmth—until the winter of the influenza epidemic. The disease took many men, women, and children that year.

Jubal and Rebekah took all the precautions they could to ensure their little ones wouldn't catch the deadly strain of flu. Despite their best efforts, the children fell ill anyway. One by one, all four children came down with it. To make matters worse, Rebekah became sick from taking care of them. The last to catch the terrible flu was Jubal. For days, the entire family teetered between life and death. Jubal slipped in and out of consciousness over the next couple of days.

After five days of fighting the influenza, his fever broke and Jubal Reeves felt feeling much better. Sadly, he was the only member of the Reeves family to recover. The grown man wept like a child when he realized his wife and four children were dead. There had been no funerals. He hadn't even buried his own family. Before Jubal's recovery, the family doctor had stopped by to check on the family. The old physician found only the elder Reeves alive. He wasn't sure that Reeves would survive, but he was hopeful. Knowing how painful it would be for the man to have to deal with the loss of his entire family, doc thought it best to bury the family and spare the poor fellow any further grief.

Family friends brought food and cleaned the cabin, but finally just left Reeves alone to grieve. There wasn't anything else anyone could do. Only time could heal him and allow him to get on with his life. But time didn't seem to help. In fact, as time went on, things only got worse. Neighbors who came to check on him reported seeing a woman's dress and children's clothes drying on the line. The local shopkeeper said Reeves had stopped in a couple of times and bought candy "for the children." One couple who stopped by to see how Jubal Reeves was doing and to bring him a pie found him finishing his supper. To their astonishment, he had set the table for six—as if his family was still alive! No one knew what to do. He seemed to be carrying on as if he still had a family. Nothing anyone said made any difference.

Finally, the minister was sent to talk to the pitiful man. After spending hours counseling Jubal Reeves, he left feeling as if his parishioner hadn't heard a word he had said. Shortly thereafter, Jubal Reeves sold some land and gave the proceeds to the local shopkeeper so that the merchant would periodically deliver food and supplies. He was seen on occasion by passersby, chopping wood and tending to other daily responsibilities, but he never left the area around his cabin. He became a recluse.

A traveler happened upon the Reeves homestead one night on his way through the mountains. As he approached the door to ask for hospitality, he heard the laughter and squeals of happy children. The man decided to go on to the next place, as he was hesitant to intrude on the family's merriment.

When he reached another cabin, a couple of miles due east, he eagerly knocked. The man of the house graciously welcomed him and asked his wife to give the weary traveler some supper. He thanked them and said he sure was glad they were so hospitable because it had been further between cabins than he had thought it would be. "What do you mean?" The traveler explained how he had planned to stop at another cabin, but he had not wanted to intrude. The man and his wife looked at each other in puzzlement before turning their attention back to their guest. "There's no other cabin nearby but the Reeves place, and Jubal lives alone. Lost his wife and kids in a big epidemic we had in these parts some years back. Never got over it, poor man," he explained.

"That can't be!" the traveler sputtered as he dropped his spoon in disbelief. "I heard a man and a woman talking and then children laughing—even giggling!"

Over the years, there were others who made the same claim— that they heard a family laughing and talking inside the cabin. Some say it was the spirits of Jubal's wife and children, back to help him cope with the physical loss of his loved ones. When he passed away, Jubal Reeves was buried next to his wife and children. Their graves are deep in the forests of the Uwharrie Mountains. Old timers still remember the tale of the phantom family.

*About these mountains...*
While most folks haven't heard of the Uwharrie Mountains, they are considered to be the oldest range on our continent. Because they are so old, they have eroded significantly. Still, this mountain range is the highest uplift in eastern North Carolina. Elevations range from 450 feet to close to 950 feet on Cedar Mountain (northeastern portion of Uwharries).

# HAUNTINGS AT THE BURGWIN-WRIGHT HOUSE

Wilmington

*A secret tunnel extends from the house down to the Cape Fear River. While its existence has been rumored for decades, the remains of the tunnel were discovered just a few years ago.*

$B$uilt around 1770 by successful merchant and planter John Burgwin, the house represents Georgian-style architecture. The land the house is built on was purchased in 1744 so a jail could be constructed on it. Wilmington's abandoned jail was used to create an outstanding stone foundation for the house. A secret tunnel extends from the home down to the Cape Fear River. While its existence has been rumored for decades, the remains of the tunnel were discovered just a few years ago.

The house itself also has an intriguing history. It was occupied in 1781 by Lord Cornwallis, who used it as his headquarters just after his defeat in the Battle of Guilford Court House. In fact, Cornwallis kept his prisoners in this dungeon until he surrendered at Yorktown.

Joshua Grainger Wright bought the house in 1799. It remained a residence until 1937, when the National Society of the Colonial Dames of America in the State of North Carolina bought the house. The women opened the house to tourists in 1950. It is considered a great example of a colonial gentleman's town residence. The house has double porches on both sides and a formal garden. Inside, visitors can see its exquisite eighteenth- and nineteenth-century furnishings.

Guests may even witness a ghost since the property is reportedly haunted, some say by the ghosts of prisoners whom Cornwallis stashed in the dungeon. This explains the soft wailing that has been heard on occasion. It sounds like it is coming from under the house. It is possible that it is a cat or the wind—or it may be souls of those poor soldiers who had the misfortune to be incarcerated here during the war. Cornwallis didn't give the men enough food and water.

They were beaten if they tried to escape or complain. The dungeon was dark, damp, and dreadful

As far as I know, the spirits of these soldiers do not venture inside the house, although it seems that some mischievous ghost must be hanging around. According to docent Ardell Tiller, something unexplainable occurs every day in a small bedroom upstairs. Tiller closes the little door to the Blue Bedroom each night before leaving, and every morning she finds it open. She says no one claims to have opened the door, and it closes tightly, so it couldn't just blow open. Tiller says that is the only strange thing that has happened since she became a docent a couple of years ago, but she has heard a story about the spinning wheel.

Some years ago there was a spinning wheel on the hearth of a room upstairs. One day when a tour reached that room, the docent began her talk on the room and its furnishings. Suddenly, the spinning wheel began turning. The tour guide was so shocked she stopped talking and walked over to the wheel. It suddenly stopped. The woman explained to the participants that the spinning wheel had been stuck in place until now. Efforts to loosen it had been unsuccessful and the women had ceased trying because they didn't want to damage the old wheel. If that wasn't strange enough, another examination of the wheel showed that it was stuck in place again. The brief, rapid turning of the wheel could never be explained. The spinning wheel is no longer displayed in that room at the Burgwin-Wright House.

*If you're going . . .*
The Burgwin-Wright House and Gardens is located at 224 Market Street (at the corner of Market and 3rd Streets), in Wilmington's Historic District. (910) 762-0570. It is the oldest museum house in southeastern North Carolina. There are several other historic homes in the area, many of them also reported to be haunted.

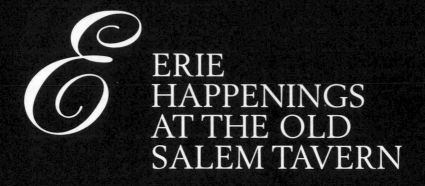

# ERIE HAPPENINGS AT THE OLD SALEM TAVERN

Winston-Salem

*Just as he started back downstairs, a shadowy figure appeared in front of him. Before the keeper could decide what to do next, the specter spoke.*

*T*he man finally got the door of the tavern open and then collapsed on the floor, barely across the threshold. The crumpled figure was taken to a room upstairs while the doctor was summoned. When the physician arrived, he sadly announced that there was nothing he could do to save the man. He was too far gone, the doctor reported. The stranger was kept as comfortable as possible until he died a few hours later. The tavern keeper and doctor looked through the few possessions he had on him, hoping to determine his identity.

They didn't find any clues and no one came looking for him. The corpse was buried on September 6, 1831, in what is now called the Stranger's Graveyard. Records lead us to believe that the man was Samuel McClary, a well-to-do merchant from Charleston. McClary was on his way to Charleston, South Carolina, from Virginia when he took ill.

In earlier days, taverns provided more than drinks and food. They also served as shelter for exhausted travelers. Since these were the days of horses and buggies, taverns also served as good spots to wait out inclement weather. Old Salem Tavern had an outstanding reputation as a worthy stop for travelers. The tavern was church-owned and staffed mostly by slaves, except for a twelve-year period from 1791 until 1803. George Washington once stayed at the tavern in 1791.

The servants began acting peculiarly shortly after the unidentified man's death. When the keeper asked what was wrong, they told him they had heard unexplainable sounds coming from the basement ever since the man had died in the tavern. The servants also complained of "cold spots" in the tavern that they had never felt before. A couple of them claimed to have been followed, although they didn't see anyone when they turned around. Despite the keeper's assurances that nothing was amiss, the servants sincerely believed the tavern was now haunted.

Something happened one night that convinced even the keeper that something was amiss at the old tavern. A servant girl ran into his office one evening and screamed that there was something in the attic. Unable to calm her, he finally promised to go have a look himself. Admittedly, the attic was rather dark and scary at night, he thought, as he looked around it. With all the recent talk by the staff about the place being haunted, it was no wonder the girl had imagined she saw or heard something. Just as he started back downstairs, a shadowy figure appeared in front of him. Before the keeper could decide what to do next, the specter spoke. He gave the startled man instructions: "Let my fiancée know of my death." He disclosed his identity as Samuel McClary and gave the address of the woman he was betrothed to in Charleston. Then he vanished as quickly as he had appeared.

The keeper did as he was instructed. He wrote the young lady about the death of Samuel McClary. Less than a month later, the woman arrived in Salem to oversee the reburial of McClary. He was moved to God's Acre and given a proper tombstone. God's Acre was first used in 1771. Today, members of the Moravian Church are still buried in this graveyard, separated in groups according to choirs: married men and widowers, married women and widows, single men and boys, single women and girls.

His fiancée also claimed his belongings, which had been stored in the attic. From that day forward, there were no more strange sounds or sightings. There were no more "cold spots." Everything went back to normal. But no one forgot what transpired before the young man was properly buried at God's Acre.

*If you're going . . .*
Lunch and dinner are still served most days of the week in the Tavern-Annex building, which was constructed in 1816. It is next door to the original tavern, which now serves as a museum. Visitors can explore the grounds of Old Salem, known as a Living History Town,

and its shops and bakery for free or pay to take a guided tour that permits entrance to most buildings (including the tavern museum) and features a short audiovisual orientation. Special events are presented seasonally. The Old Salem Children's Museum, Old Salem Toy Museum, and Museum of Early Southern Decorative Arts are also located at Old Salem.

Old Salem is southwest of the intersection of I-40 Business and Hwy. 52, near downtown Winston-Salem. 900 Old Salem Road. Brown highway signs posted along all major highways will show you the way. The signs will direct you to the visitors center parking lot. For more information, call toll-free (888) 653-7253 or (336) 721-7350, or visit www.salem.org.

# WRATH OF OLD SQUIRE

Benson/Four Oaks

*Trying to keep his heart from beating out of his chest, the slave slowly answered, "I think I seen 'im near the barn early this morning but that was the last I seen of 'im."*

I n May 1820, a mean man known to his slaves as Master Lynch took one of his slaves, Old Squire, to the banks of Mill Creek to clear and cultivate the soil. He wanted to see if the land could be made to produce a fine cotton crop. If the experiment yielded promising results, the plantation owner planned to bring more men to ready the ground for planting. Lynch was frustrated at the slow progress that was being made. He took his frustration out on the poor slave. Lynch stood over Old Squire like a tyrant, shouting at him to work harder. "Is that the best you can do? Why my dog can dig better than that!"

Anger boiled up in the slave as he endured repeated insults and non-stop commands. Finally, he couldn't take anymore. In a fit of rage, Old Squire raised the hoe high up in the air, swung around, and brought it down on his master's head. Lynch screamed in pain as the tool hit him squarely on the side of his head. Instinctively, he raised his arms up to the wound but fell to the ground before his hands reached his head.

Old Squire carefully leaned down and inspected the crumpled body. There was no sign of life. He gently kicked the man's leg, but there was no response. After a more thorough exam, Old Squire realized the man was dead. Oh good Lord, what had he done! He had sure enough gone and killed Master Lynch. Old Squire looked all around and soon realized no one had witnessed what had happened. He quickly dragged the corpse under the bridge and started digging. When he had finally dug a hole big enough to conceal the body, the slave half-carried, half-rolled Lynch into the small pit. When the burial was finished, Old Squire went back to the creek bank and continued to hoe the cotton as if nothing had happened!

At the end of the day he returned to the plantation and had supper. Someone knocked on his door as he was retiring for the evening. It was Lynch's oldest son, inquiring as to the whereabouts of his father. "Sorry to bother you, Old Squire, but my father hasn't come home and we're asking everyone if they've seen him today. He left this morning and no one seems to know where he went." Trying to keep his heart from beating out of his chest, the slave slowly answered, "I think I seen 'im near the barn early this morning but that was the last I seen of 'im."

Despite an extensive search, the body was never discovered. No one ever knew about that day until Old Squire confessed on his deathbed. There have been reports of strange sounds, best described as "moaning." Also, whenever anyone tried to cross the Mill Creek Bridge carrying a light, it went out—even when there was no wind or breeze in the air, even if it was a flashlight. The light would always work properly once over the bridge. One version of the story includes two lights that look like lanterns that bob across the bridge as if being carried by two different people. Some folks like to believe this is Master Lynch and Old Squire, still trying to get that land readied for planting.

*If you're going . . .*
Mill Creek is in Johnston County, about fourteen miles south of Smithfield on 701. At Shaw's Creek Road, make a left turn. In about a mile you'll see two bridges. The area is pretty swampy nowadays, so beware, and I'm not sure which bridge is reportedly haunted or if the original bridge is long gone.

# THALIAN HALL SPECTERS

Wilmington

Wilmington needed a theater and it had to be big enough to accommodate large crowds since the booming port city already boasted over six thousand residents. The facility also needed to be grand enough to attract celebrities and first-class performers. When it opened in 1858, everyone agreed that Thalian Hall more than fulfilled its obligations. The theater was, and still is, an architectural marvel. Its style and splendor have been copied by other architects, including the man who designed the famous Ford Theater in Washington. Out of the thousands of actors who have performed at Thalian Hall, more than a few have claimed they felt an "unseen presence" backstage.

It's certainly possible, since there are some actors who like the theater so well that they refuse to leave—even after their deaths! The theater is reputedly haunted by two ghosts, believed to be the spirits of Maude Adams and James O'Neill. Both performed at the theater, although not in the same production. It's believed that Adams is the protector (or guardian angel) of Thalian Hall and O'Neill is the mischievous one, responsible for moving items or playing with the stage lights.

One time when a workman was above the main stage, fixing lights on the second grid, he laid down a tool next to him. Later, when he reached for it, it was gone. The tool turned up on the lower level, where no one had been working. It couldn't have fallen without making some kind of noise. There have been other accounts of finding tools or props where they shouldn't be. Sometimes, workmen or actors are positive that they didn't leave an item where it was found.

The lights are dimmer lights, which means in addition to flipping on and off, they can also be turned from low to bright. On occasion, the lights have inexplicably gone from low to bright and bright to low and from off to on and on to off. This is especially hard to explain.

The most intriguing experience occurred many years ago during a performance. One of the actresses had to make a quick change into an Edwardian costume that had dozens of tiny buttons that had to be fastened. In order to help the actress, the wardrobe manager always buttoned as many of them as possible while still leaving enough unfastened so the girl could put the dress on without difficulty. After she did her part, the wardrobe manager always put the outfit over the back of a chair in the actress's dressing room.

During a particularly hectic performance night, the manager realized she had forgotten to get the dress ready for the actress, who was about to finish her scene. Knowing the girl would dash offstage to change, the wardrobe manager hurried to get the dress. When she couldn't find it anywhere that it should be, she desperately ran to the girl's dressing room to see if it just might be there. When she flung open the door, the costume was on the chair. Amazingly, the dress was neatly pressed and partly buttoned—just the way she usually prepared it for the actress.

Thinking the girl must have taken the initiative, the busy woman dismissed the event and carried on with her duties that evening. After the performance, when she praised the girl for her initiative with the costume, the wardrobe manager learned that the actress had not readied the dress for the costume change. A quick investigation revealed no one else admitted to helping with the outfit. In fact, no one associated with the production knew anything about this necessary preparation. No one seemed to know how the costume got into the dressing room!

Stacy Edmunds, an administrative assistant at Thalian Hall, has also heard this story, but she doesn't believe a ghost was responsible for the costume incident because she doesn't think ghosts are interactive. Edmunds believes ghosts have left a powerful impression in space and time because they were such vibrant and energetic people when they were alive. Those attuned to this energy can even see them. She's a believer because she has seen a ghost!

It happened at Bessie's, a popular bar in Wilmington's Historic District. The Front Street hang out was formerly the Orton Hotel. Stacy was in the ladies' restroom when she was startled to see a black man, who appeared to be in his early twenties, wearing a string bow tie, entering the ladies room. Before she could ask him what he was doing there, he walked right past her through the wall! Edmunds figures he worked in the kitchen when the building was the Orton Hotel. According to old floorplans of the hotel, the bathrooms at Bessie's are in close proximity to the hotel's kitchen.

Although Stacy Edmunds has never seen the ghosts of Thalian Hall, there have been sightings on the third floor of the theater. Those who have seen the ghosts describe a seated man (James O'Neill) wearing a dark suit. A woman (Maude Adams) is seen walking around in a black dress with a big bustle. Some patrons seated on the third floor of the theater have sworn they felt "cold spots." Some experts believe that cold spots are the result of a spirit using up all the body heat and warmth in given area. So, if there is a dramatic drop in the temperature, it is believed that a ghost is present, even if it cannot seen.

In 1990, the performing arts hall underwent a major $5.5 million revitalization effort. Today, the lobby is where the back of the building was originally. The entrance used to be on Princess Street, but it was moved to Chestnut Street when the 25,000-square-foot extension was completed. The new part also houses the box office, some offices, a studio theatre, dressing rooms, and stage support rooms. Photographs of famous performers who have appeared at the theater hang in the new lobby.

Even though changes on the third level were minimal, mainly bringing it up to code, the ghosts haven't been seen since the renovations. Maybe there have been too many changes for Adams and O'Neill to continue to call it home, or maybe they are satisfied that Thalian Hall is being well maintained and they have moved on. Or have they? A woman in a tour group a few weeks prior to my visit claimed to have felt a presence, according to a young man working in the box office. Miss Edmunds admits she sometimes experiences creepy sensations on the third floor. "There is a really old, antique couch and you will start to feel a little queasy if you stand in front of it long enough," the young woman explained.

*About the theater . . .*
The theater is named after Thalia, the Greek muse of comedy and poetry. If you're interested in seeing what the resident specters looked like when they were alive, there is a portrait of Miss Maude Adams on the third floor as Lady Robbie in "The Little Minister." It's dated September 23, 1912. There is also a photo of Mr. James O'Neill when he played the Count of Monte Cristo, taken January 2, 1902.

Thalian Hall is part of the League of Historic American Theatres, the Association of Performing Arts, and the North Carolina Presenters Consortium. Tours of the 150-year-old theater edifice are given by appointment. 310 Chesnut Street, Wilmington. For more information, call toll-free (800) 523-2820 or (910) 343-3660 or visit www.thalianhall.com

# PROFESSOR WILLIAMS, I PRESUME?

Chapel Hill

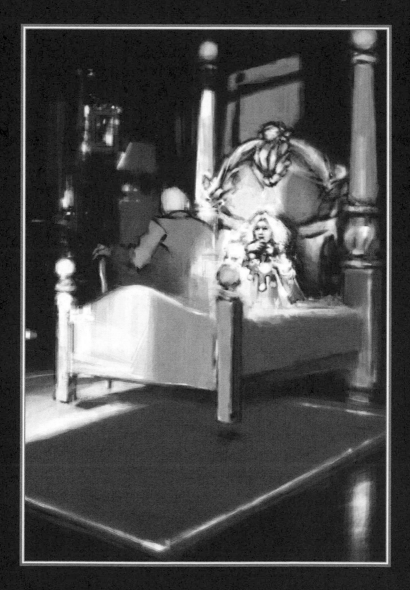

*"My sister said he would just sit on the edge of her bed and talk with her,"* Williams said. *"It was not a scary presence. It wasn't threatening. But we all felt it."*

Chapel Hill has many historic homes, several of which are reportedly haunted. This particular dwelling, originally an 1840s farmhouse, is located at 610 E. Rosemary Street. When Horace Williams bought it, he was attracted by its Octagon Room, parlor, and large front porch. A previous owner had made these renovations in the 1880s. Williams was a distinguished professor of philosophy and chairman of the Philosophy Department at the University of North Carolina at Chapel Hill. He died of natural causes in 1940 and willed the house to the school with one stipulation—that it not be altered by modern renovations. Through the years, the house has been home to many tenants.

Catherine Berryhill Williams, Special Events Coordinator for University of North Carolina President Molly Broad, was one such inhabitant. For four years, when she was a child, she and her family lived in the house. Because of strange incidents that occurred in the house, none of her friends wanted to come over and play, Williams recalled during an interview with the *Daily Tar Heel*. Though Williams claims she doesn't believe in ghosts, she did admit that she and her family felt a presence in the house.

What's more ominous is that things were often found out of place and no one admitted to moving them. "In the evening, my mother would bank the fire before she went to bed and she would place the fire utensils on one side of the fireplace," Williams said. "And in the morning they would always be on the other side of the fireplace."

It's popularly believed that the ghost is Horace Williams, who loved the house so much that he made sure that no significant changes could be made to it, as per his will. Maybe he stayed around to make sure his orders were followed. Williams said her sister claimed to have had several conversations with the ghost of Horace Williams. "My sister said he would sit on the edge of her bed and talk softly with her," Williams said. "It was not a scary presence. It wasn't threatening. But we all felt it."

The Horace Williams House is part of the Chapel Hill Historic District and is now home to the Chapel Hill Preservation Society. The school still owns the house, but the Preservation Society leases it to use as their headquarters. Society Director Catherine Frank says that she has not witnessed any unusual occurrences but that her predecessor claimed that a metal container that was kept on the mantel was often found in a different spot from where it was carefully placed. She says they do have trouble periodically with one of the lights, but Frank believes that it has more to do with the old wiring than with ghosts.

But how do you explain the rocking chair? When the caretaker for the property was interviewed a couple of years ago on a local radio program, he swore that he has seen a rocking chair move like someone is sitting in it rocking. He says the movement is so regular that it cannot be explained away by wind or fans. The chair clearly moves as if someone were sitting in it rocking back and forth, but no one is in the chair—at least no human being!

*If you're going . . .*
The Horace Williams House is in Chapel Hill's Historic District, 610 E. Rosemary Street. In the early days, the dwelling was a plain farmhouse. The school once owned it but later sold it to one of their professors, Benjamin Hedrick, in 1855 for $300. Hedrick is one who added the Octagon Room and also made several other renovations to the house. Horace Williams bought the residence in 1897 and lived there until his death in 1940. The university once again owns the property but has leased it to the Chapel Hill Preservation Society (www.chapelhillpreservation.com) since 1973.

# PINK LADY AT THE GROVE PARK INN

Asheville

*"It got so bad, I couldn't work up the courage to go in [the room], even though I tried. In fact, to my last day at the hotel, I never did go back there—sent my boys instead."*

*U*nder orders from his doctor, Edwin W. Grove, founder and owner of Grove's Pharmacy and Paris Medical Company of St. Louis, Missouri, spent summers in Asheville in the late 1800s. His physician believed the mountain climate would be good therapy for Grove's chronic bronchitis. Not only did Grove's ailment improve, but he also fell in love with the area and decided to build a luxury hotel in Asheville.

"The idea was to build a big home where every modern convenience could be found, but with all the old-fashioned qualities of genuineness with no sham . . . " stated Fred L. Seely, E.W. Grove's son-in-law and co-developer.

The Grove Park Inn is certainly worthy of its standing on the National Register of Historic Places. Constructed in 1913, the impressive edifice has accommodated many famous people such as Harry Houdini, Richard Nixon, Thomas Edison, and F. Scott Fitzgerald. Many of these dignitaries and celebrities have shared thoughts that are now engraved in the stones that comprise the lobby.

Grove envisioned building to be one of the world's greatest resorts, and there is no doubt the award-winning Grove Park Inn has achieved that goal. Sitting majestically above Asheville, the sprawling retreat was constructed with granite stones, some weighing as much as ten thousand pounds. The inside of it is just as grand as the exterior. The Grove Park Inn has ten floors, which hold over five hundred rooms and suites, as well as fifty thousand square feet of meeting space (including two ballrooms). The inn provides golf, tennis, two pools, an indoor sports center, shops and boutiques, a nightclub, and fine dining. Additionally, a forty-thousand-square-foot state-of-the-art spa was recently completed.

But what has drawn many guests and visitors for over a half

century is not just the amenities but also the Pink Lady. The legend starts in the 1920s when a pretty young girl in a pink ball gown plummeted to her death from room 545. It has never been determined whether the tragedy occurred because she leaned over too far and lost her balance, because she meant to take her life, or because she was pushed. Regardless of how she died, many swear her spirit lingers.

Over the years, numerous guests and hotel staff have reported extraordinary experiences. Many claim to have seen the figure in the pale pink dress. According to them, it vanishes just as quickly as it appears. Some witnesses say it is more like a thick, pinkish smoke that takes on the conceptual shape of a woman rather than a definitive womanly figure. Others claim that what they see is unmistakably a female specter. Still others say they have sensed, rather than seen, the apparition. These witnesses say she has sat down on the bed next to them; they have sensed her spirit lagging just behind them when walking down a hallway, and they have even felt themselves being led by the arm.

The elevator is sometimes summoned to the fifth floor, which happens to be the floor from which the girl fell to her death. When the elevator doors open, no one is waiting to get onto the elevator. Lights turn on and off by themselves, as if switched on by an invisible hand. Empty guest rooms and bathrooms have been found locked from the inside, which is impossible unless someone is inside to lock the door from that side. Keys cannot unlock these rooms, so doors must be taken off the hinges in order to get them open.

A painter who was employed by the hotel from the 1950s through the 1980s said that "back in the late fifties or early sixties, the hotel used to shut down during the winter months and that's when we caught up on painting. One cloudy, gloomy day, I was checking on some of my guys' work. As I got closer to room 545, I got cold chills that got worse the closer I came to the door. It got so bad, I couldn't work up the courage to go in [the room], even though I tried. In fact, to my last day at the hotel, I never did go back there—sent my boys instead."

63

*The Great Hall of Grove Park Inn Resort.*

The engineering facilities manager also reported a strange sensation in 1995: "I was on my way to check a recent bathtub resurfacing in room 545. As I approached the room, my hair suddenly lifted from my scalp and the tiny hairs on my arms stood on end. Simultaneously, I felt a very uncomfortable, cold rush across my whole body. I didn't go in, haven't gone back, and don't ever intend to."

The painter had long since retired when the engineering manager was hired, so neither man knew about the other's experience. The strange encounters are not restricted to employees. Many guests have also had them, including the two-year-old son of a Florida college professor, the Kitty Hawk Chief of Police, and the President of the National Federation of Press Women. One might attribute some of these events to elaborate childish pranks or overactive imaginations, but these things have happened when there have only been a few guests staying at the inn, and they were all accounted for. Longtime employees are unlikely to make up such tales and have actually been the most reluctant to discuss their ghostly experiences.

In fact, hotel management used to discourage employees from talking about the ghost. They considered it bad for business. When, on the contrary, curiosity seekers who had heard rumors of a ghost began to flock to Grove Park in hopes of spotting the wispy figure, the inn changed its stance. Management even went so far as to hire local ghost hunter Joshua Warren to investigate the Pink Lady in 1995. Warren spent the first six months of 1996 investigating the resort and interviewing nearly fifty people who claimed to have had unusual experiences or encounters with the Pink Lady. After his study of Grove Park Inn, he wrote *Haunted Asheville*, which documents his findings.

Just how does one determine whether a ghost is hanging around? For starters, Warren spent different nights in various rooms at the inn. Three men sometimes assisted him. Mark-Ellis Bennett, who is a restoration artist at the inn, was in charge of conducting ultrasonic and subsonic audio recordings. Tim Vandenberghe, who is employed as a general technician at the resort, served as a field research assistant and was in charge of the infrared night vision scope. Tim Pedersen, Grove Park Inn general technician, also assisted in the investigation.

Strong, unexplainable, electromagnetic energy was measured in many places within the inn. Two photographs revealed "ghostly mist" in a chair and in the background of an identification photo of Warren and Pedersen. One night Warren and Vandenberghe staked out Elaine's, the hotel nightclub. On that occasion, they used a Van de Graaff electrostatic generator. The machine measured significant electrical discharges. Vandenberghe also reported he saw a "white streak of illumination" while he was looking through the infrared night vision scope.

At the end of Joshua Warren's scientific examination of Grove Park Inn, he came to the conclusion that room 545 is the most haunted locale in the hotel. Obviously, because this is the room the mysterious woman was staying in when she fell from the balcony to her death.

Media Relations Director Dave Thompsky told me that guests occupy room 545 eight nights out of ten. Most leave saying they had some kind of Pink Lady encounter. Thompsky is quick to point out that she is not harmful, merely forlorn or playful. When I interviewed him, he said that the last sighting occurred less than two months ago.

But who is the Pink Lady? Who is this girl who died so many years ago and still haunts the premises today? Why was she at the hotel? What happened the night of her death? No one has any idea. Unfortunately, guest records are not available from that far back. Thompsky agreed that Warren's research was very thorough and that if he could not find the origin of the Pink Lady, it most likely won't be discovered. If you want to see the Pink Lady of Grove Park Inn, the best chance is around midnight in the late fall and winter. The best places are room 545 and in the main part of the inn. Even if you don't encounter the specter, you're sure to enjoy your visit at the legendary Grove Park Inn Resort.

*If you're going* . . .
Grove Park Inn Resort is located at 290 Macon Avenue, Asheville, NC 28807. Call (800) 438-0050 or (828) 252-5585, or visit www. groveparkinn.com.

For more information on what Asheville has to offer, call the Asheville Chamber of Commerce Convention & Visitors Bureau at (800) 257-1300 or (828) 258-6101 or visit www.ashevillechamber. org.

# EVEN GHOSTS LIKE A GOOD GAME OF POOL

Asheville

*Family members and more than a few guests have gone so far as to say that they have felt they were not alone in their bedrooms. They felt some kind of supernatural presence.*

*I*n 1892, Samuel Harrison Reed purchased eighteen acres and built an enormous home with ten fireplaces, sixty-two windows, and a turret. Samuel Reed and his wife had nine children. Sadly, five of the children didn't live long enough to become adults. His wife also died prematurely at age fifty. Less than a year later, Samuel Reed passed away. The four remaining children were sent to live with relatives and the house was rented out for a while and then sold.

The estate had many owners through the years. Ultimately, it was abandoned for nearly a decade, which resulted in significant deterioration. In 1972, the city decided to condemn it. But Marge Turcot, president of the Preservation Society of Asheville and Buncombe County, decided the mansion was worth saving. She and her husband bought the run-down house and began restoring it.

The first night they stayed there, the Turcots heard loud footsteps on the back stairs. When Marge checked on her children, she found them all fast asleep. From that night on, the family often heard unexplainable footsteps on the stairs. The Turcots also claim that bedroom doors open and close on their own.

However, the most fascinating thing is what happens behind closed doors in the game room. The sounds of a good game of pool being played have been heard, including the clinking of balls as they bounce off one another and the sounds of balls racing across the padded table. Yet no human source has ever been discovered in the billiards room when a family member investigates the noises. So where is the unmistakable noise of a pool game coming from? Samuel Reed loved a good game of pool, so many are convinced that he is responsible for the noises.

The renovated property became a bed and breakfast in 1985 and has comfortably accommodated many guests since that time. Some guests, however, got more than they expected. They claim to have seen and heard many creepy things—books leaping off the bookshelves, heavy footsteps, the sounds of children playing, strange sounds coming from the empty attic, and lights turning on or off, as if by magic. Family members and more than a few guests have gone so far as to say that they have felt they were not alone in their bedrooms. Many believe the only explanation is that the spirits of the Reed family, including Samuel, his wife, and the five children who died in the house, have chosen to remain in their former residence.

*If you're going . . .*
The Victorian mansion was built in 1892 by Samuel Harrison Reed. Reed was one of Vanderbilt's lawyers. He lived in the home until his death. The property became a bed and breakfast several years ago. It is listed on the National Register of Historic Places and has also been declared a local historic property by the Historic Resources Commission. 119 Dodge Street, Asheville (located in Biltmore Village). (828) 274-1604.

# UNSTAGED PRODUCTIONS AT AYCOCK AUDITORIUM

Greensboro

*"Next, the lights flashed on and off while a white kind of apparition, smokelike thing passed across the stage and came down the steps and was walking toward me."*

*L*ocated on the corner of Spring Garden and Tate Streets, the Aycock Auditorium was built on the University of North Carolina Greensboro campus (located in central North Carolina). The college bought the land and tore down an old house that was on the property in order to accommodate the theater. The spirit of a woman named Jane Aycock, who hanged herself in the attic, supposedly haunted the house that was razed.

Apparently, Jane has taken up residence in the school building. She has been spotted by the auditorium manager and by theater students. She is notorious for turning lights on and off in the auditorium. In fact, a switch on the lighting board is labeled "Jane's dimmer." Even though males and females have witnessed strange incidents credited to Jane Aycock, no female has ever seen the specter. Jane only reveals herself to men.

Theater professor Tom Behm remains spooked by his encounter with Jane. In 1988, he was directing the musical *Bye, Bye Birdie* and had accidentally left his briefcase in the theater. It was late at night when he returned for it, so most of the lights were off. When Behm reached the middle of the auditorium, stage lights came on. Next, the lights flashed on and off while a "white kind of apparition, smoke-like thing passed across the stage and came down the steps and was walking toward me." The professor admits he grabbed his briefcase and quickly exited the building. He says he has not been inside the theater alone since that night.

Theater major Jeff Neubauer and a friend locked up the theater one night in 1995. As they stood outside the building, the youths noticed a "very fair, white-looking woman with light-colored hair" walking past the window. Jeff figured it had to be Jane. There was no other logical explanation.

That same year, Aycock auditorium manager Lyman Collins

met Jane. Having heard the stories, he was curious as to their va-lidity. Collins boldly picked Halloween night to find out whether Jane existed. He waited until everyone was gone and then headed for a spot Jane supposedly was fond of on the third balcony. Collins stayed a long time before giving up his quest to meet Jane. As he was locking the building, he heard the sound of piano keys. His heart thumping, Lyman raced into the auditorium and towards the piano. The noise stopped before he got near the piano, which had been temporarily moved from its usual place into the aisle while a painter finished working. The theater manager is sure the music was Jane letting him know the piano didn't belong there. After his encounter, he sees her as a helpful spirit. Many others do not share his sentiment. While some agree Jane is merely mischievous, others consider her downright unnerving or scary.

In September 1997, UNCG senior Michael Marlowe saw Jane. It was during the staging of the musical *Tommy*. He was in the base-ment when he saw "something in white walking up the stairway into the orchestra pit." Jeff Neubauer, who had once seen Jane walking past a window, had another encounter with Jane. This time it was much more intense. Neubauer had been sent down to the basement to find a prop needed for the school's current production, *Phantom of the Opera*. While leaning down peering through boxes of props, the student felt a hand on his shoulder. The startled young man jumped up and swung around, but no one was there! Although Neubauer says he is not scared of the apparition, he flatly refuses to go into the basement anymore.

A former drama professor, Raymond Taylor, had an interesting experience one long hot summer. He remembered having to sort and stack costumes on humid days because the building lacked air conditioning at that time. He would later find those same garments scattered about the area rather than neatly sorted and stacked as he had left them.

During spring 2006, Western Carolina University Professor Al Proffit was invited to Greensboro by a UNCG group to investigate the ghost. Proffit, who is a ghost hunter in his spare time, jumped at the chance. He interviewed folks who had experiences, including

*View of Aycock Auditorium as seen from the balcony.*

costume shop supervisor Julian Cheek and former technical crew manager Erin Doll Stevie. Each recounted stories of lights and radios mysteriously coming on, of sewing machines spinning without an operator, of feeling hands on shoulders when no one is there, and of hearing footsteps on an empty stage. At the end of his investigation, Profitt could not say whether the auditorium is truly haunted. He said that further tests, such as using electromagnetic meters, would be necessary before any conclusion could be reached. But don't tell that to all the students and faculty at UNCG who have had eerie encounters with the ghost of Jane Aycock.

The best chance of seeing Jane is to be in the building alone the basement, if you dare. . . .

*About the University...*
The University of North Carolina at Greensboro was founded by legislative enactment on February 18, 1891. It was decided that the school would be established in Greensboro because it is near the geographical center of the state. The University of North Carolina at Greensboro now offers more than 150 undergraduate and graduate degree programs. 1000 Spring Garden Street, Greensboro, NC 27403.

# HANGING AT HELEN'S BRIDGE

Asheville

*L*egend has it that in the early 1900s, a woman named Helen lived with her young daughter in a small house located near a bridge and a secluded estate on Asheville's Beaucatcher Mountain. The little girl used to slip off to the abandoned castle to play. One afternoon while she was there, a fire occurred in the room the child was in and she died in the blaze. The death of her only child devastated Helen. Unable to bear the loss, the heartbroken woman hanged herself from the old bridge.

Through the years, sightings of Helen have been reported on the grounds of the castle, bridge, and surrounding area. Locals say that you may spot the apparition if you park your car under this bridge and call out "Helen, come forth!" three times. If she touches the vehicle, a tiny, permanent mark will appear there. Beware! If you see Helen, it is reported that you'll have car trouble on the way home.

It is even reported that Helen haunts the castle where her only child was killed. Known as Zealandia, the castle was built in 1889 by John Evans Brown. He came from Pennsylvania to Asheville in the mid-1800s for a visit and fell in love with the mountain community. Brown bought 168 acres on Beaucatcher Mountain, but his wandering spirit wasn't quite ready to settle down. He went West during the Gold Rush but returned home empty-handed. Soon afterwards, he was off again, this time to New Zealand to try his hand at sheep farming.

He met with much success in this endeavor and returned to Asheville a very rich man in 1884. He also brought back a bride, the adopted daughter of a wealthy merchant. Brown started construction on his dream home and when it was completed in 1889, he

*This undated photograph shows the exterior of Zealandia before it was torn down.*

named it Zealandia, in honor of the time he had happily spent in New Zealand. The owner lived in the castle until his death, a mere six years later.

At that time, Brown's heirs sold Zealandia to O.D. Revell, who sold it to Sir Philip S. Henry. Born in Australia, Henry was a diplomat and scholar who received many accolades. His wife, Violet Lewisohn Henry, died in the Windsor Hotel fire in New York City just before the couple was to move to Asheville. The guests were all told to leave the premises because a fire had broken out. Despite the tremendous risk, Mrs. Henry went back into the hotel to get some valuable jewelry she had left in their room. The ceiling caved in and killed her.

Some believe Zealandia's ghost is not Helen, but Violet Henry. They believe that Mrs. Henry's spirit lingered to watch and protect her family, and later, other families who resided in Sir Henry's estate. During the thirty years Sir Henry lived in the castle, he doubled the size of the estate and built an English Tudor mansion and a carriage bridge leading to it.

*A rare look at the interior of the house during the time Sir Philip Henry resided there. The house was filled with priceless antiques and art.*

Sir Henry was an art lover and collector and founded the Asheville Art Association and Museum in 1930. The multi-level museum was open to the public with no admission cost. It housed rare and priceless items, such as Renaissance paintings, goblets used by the Incas during banquets, an original manuscript of the Torah, axes used by the Crusaders, and Ming dynasty vases. Sadly, this wonderful facility was torn down years later to make way for I-240.

Upon Sir Henry's death in 1933, his two daughters, Violet and Lenore, inherited the estate. The sisters married two brothers who served in the British military. During the war, Zealandia was used as an officer's club by the Air Force. Lenore's husband was killed in the war and she sold her half of Zealandia to her sister, Violet. After the war, Violet Henry Maconochie and her husband tried to sell the castle because of the enormous tax burden, but no one was interested, so they had it torn down. The English Tudor mansion Sir Henry built on his estate was left intact, and the Maconochies lived there before they eventually sold it to the Dixons.

The Dixons used it as a spring retreat from their main residence in Miami. Like Sir Philip Henry, they were art enthusiasts, but their collection leaned more to furniture, including Marie Antoinette's bed and the throne of Emperor Maximilian. As for Zealandia's ghost, the Dixons and Henry's daughters all claim to have seen it, even after the castle was torn down. Mrs. Dixon continued to live on the estate after her husband's death in 1969. She believed that the ghost was none other than her late husband.

Another version of this legend is that Helen was the mistress of one of the owners of the castle. She became pregnant and he refused to acknowledge that it was his baby. The gentleman wouldn't have anything more to do with the young lady after she told him she was pregnant with his child. Helen felt very alone and extremely despondent after she was abandoned by her love, so she hanged herself from the bridge.

The mansion is no longer the scene for grand parties with guest lists that included wealthy and influential citizens such as the Biltmores, who were entertained by top-notch performers such as George Gershwin. Through the years, the estate has dwindled from 168 acres to a mere sixteen. A fire destroyed the horse stables in 1981. Since 1984, the sixty-two-room structure has housed the executive offices of Peppertree Resorts. Employees often report hearing inexplicable noises, feeling cold spots, and seeing file folders leap out of file drawers and mail fly out of mail slots. Peppertree Resorts sold it to Equivest Finance, Inc. in 1999. Since it is privately owned, Zealandia is not open to visitors.

*About the bridge . . .*
Some years ago, the Department of Transportation declared the aged bridge (also known as Helen's Bridge and Zealandia's Bridge, 1898) on Vance Gap Road unsafe and considered replacing it with a modern structure. The Asheville Historic Resources Commission and the Preservation Society, as well as some devoted individuals, played a significant role in saving and restoring the bridge. The bridge is on top of Beaucatcher Mountain. Turn right off Tunnel Road, just before the tunnel, onto a little road. Stay on the road up the mountain to a stop sign. Turn right and then take another right. There is a damaged gate and fence, protecting what's left of Zealandia Castle (1889). You'll see the bridge on your left. The area is rather overgrown so be careful. And be sure not to trespass.

# THE CORPSE IN CHAMBERS HALL

Charlotte

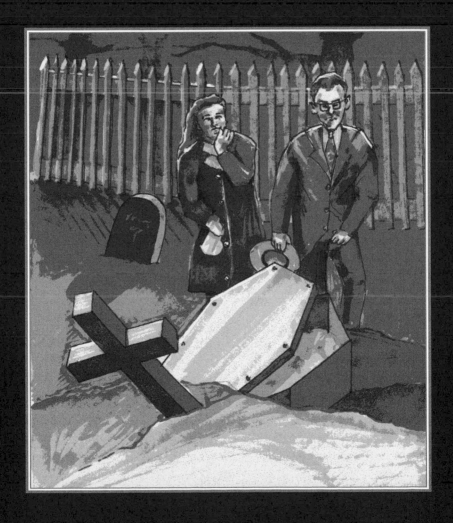

*According to the legend, the medical students, not having access to bodies otherwise destined for Potter's Field, as is the case now, were required to furnish their own cadavers, which they did by watching for interments in the local cemetery.*

*D*avidson College, located outside Charlotte in the township of Davidson, was established in 1837. Fifty-six years later, the North Carolina Medical College was founded as part of Davidson College, becoming the first chartered medical college in the state. When Davidson College professor Dr. John Peter Monroe became president of the medical school in 1896, he bought a small piece of land from Davidson College and built a three-story building to house the North Carolina Medical College. Cadavers were kept in the basement and the anatomy lab was located on the top floor. Several years later the medical school moved to 6th and Church Streets and the building became the Churchill Apartments Hotel.

In those days, a Davidson student paid $75 a year in tuition and an additional $80 for room and board. Reportedly, if students could provide cadavers they were exempt from paying tuition. In 1889, there were only two students at the medical school, but by 1904 there were nearly eighty-five students. As enrollment increased, so did the need for cadavers. An issue of *The Davidsonian* from 1960 has a story about how Sam A. Thompson confessed that he began exhuming corpses in 1899 when four medical students boarded with his family for the school year. He revealed that the snatched bodies were delivered to the school late at night. Thompson says he kept track of recent burials and joined students to exhume the bodies.

A mule-drawn carriage was used to transport the corpses to the school. The grave robber recounted a close call they had one night. The small group was on their way back to campus with a freshly exhumed cadaver when they came upon some men on the side of the road. The men stared at the corpse, which was illuminated by the moonlight. The quick-thinking driver turned and shouted back,

*Main building of North Carolina Medical College, 1898.*

"Come on and sit up now! You're not that drunk!" The ruse worked and they went on to deliver their grisly load.

The school has steadfastly denied any knowledge of these activities. However, the following letter, published in *The Charlotte Observer* on Sunday, December 4, 1949, further supports that grave robbing by medical students really happened. A former Davidson College student, Walter Dumas, wrote the letter to prominent Charlotte citizen Howard B. Arbuckle Jr. The article includes a photograph of Arbuckle holding a skull sent by Dumas. (Author's note: Grammar and punctuation are as the letter appeared in the newspaper.)

81

Dear Howard:

Through the courtesy of John Williams—"Shorty"—who is now in San Francisco with his work with the Extension Division of the University of Pennsylvania, I have been given your address. May I presume on our long though interrupted acquaintance and our mutual interest in Beta chapter of Pi Kappa Alpha to ask you to perform a small task for me?

Under a separate cover I am sending to you by parcel post a skull, which I shall appreciate your kindness in presenting with such suitable ceremony as may be indicated, to the chapter, in my name.

This is no ordinary skull. At the time I was a student at Davidson, there was a legend that somewhere about the turn of the century when Davidson had a Medical School, later moved, I believe, to Charlotte, and still later to Charlottesville, where it became the nucleus of the University of Virginia, the anatomy laboratory was in the building which in my day [was] the Biology laboratory and (strange coincidence) the College Infirmary.

According to the legend, the medical students, not having access to bodies otherwise destined for Potter's Field, as is the case now, were required to furnish their own cadavers, which they did by watching for interments in the local cemetery and visiting it for their surreptitious purposes. On one occasion they converted to their own use the body of an old Negro man. This man was the beloved retainer of a well-known family of the "White Folks," who, finding that the grave had been robbed, set the local authorities in motion. The students got wind of the impending blow, with the result that as the Sheriff came in the front door of the laboratory with his deputies and a search warrant, the students went out the back, taking "Archibald" with them. They climbed to the attic of the old Chambers Building, made their way out into the superstructure of the portico, which was supported by the famous old column, and dropped their burden down one of the columns and added a quantity of lime to destroy the evidence.

So went the story when I was a student. It had never been verified so far as we knew. Curiosity got the better of Skinny Campbell

(Ernest G., as I remember it) and me. Skinny, you may remember, was the son of Mrs. Campbell, a widow who operated a boarding house next door to Mrs. W.D. Vinson's, which was home to me for four years. We knew that there had been attempts to descend the inside of the columns but always unsuccessfully because schoolmates of the would-be adventurers had always poured buckets of water down on the explorers, or dropped burning newspapers, or otherwise succeeded in rendering the attempts abortive, all in the spirit of fun, of course.

Skinny and I, swearing each other to secrecy, decided to make a thorough search and in doing so avoid the pitfalls which had beset our predecessors of several years before. Consequently a Saturday afternoon was selected when there was some particularly interesting athletic event in progress on Sprunt Field and the campus was otherwise deserted. We took a heavy rope, flashlights, and newspapers to the top of the columns under the low roof and matched to see who would have the honor of making the first descent. Skinny won. Fearing "black damp," we dropped burning paper down a column to be sure there was an adequate oxygen supply (thereby contributing to its rapid exhaustion), secured the rope to the roof beams and dropped the end down a column where the telephone-post-like piling which was centered in the hollow shaft of the brown stone column had been burned out in the previous attempts, and Skinny went down. Result: nothing. I went down the next column and found the skull, which I am forwarding to you.

When the success of our venture became known, it naturally created a mild sensation on the campus, was written up as a lead story in *The Davidsonian* (this was the initial year of that publication), was made the theme of a story in *Davidson Magazine*, a literary periodical which may not now survive, and because of its oddity was the subject of a brief story carried by the Associated Press wires. I received many clippings from friends all over the country. A few days later Skinny went down another column and found the remains of the rest of the body, which had, allegedly, been covered with lime. The skull had shown no evidence of such treatment. He found one forearm and hand with the tendons partially intact. A later exploration of the other columns brought negative results.

That's the story, poorly told (and abominably typed).

The skull has never been cleaned up and is in the condition in which it was found except for smoke stains on the inner side of the cranium, the latter being the result of a practical joke on Alexander, the fine old Negro who took care of my room in Chambers and came in early each morning to build a fire in the fireplace so that we might have a warm room in which to dress. It was our custom to hang our clothing on a chair near the fireplace to reduce the shock of diving into cold clothes in our rush to make chapel on time. On the occasion in question Alex had laid the fire. He turned around to find seated in the chair beside him a figure with a grinning candle-lighted skull. We made our own fire for several weeks.

It was my long intention to send the skull to Beta chapter when my son could be emissary when he entered Davidson. The best-laid plans, etc., and my son chose to follow me into military profession, and was graduated from West Point in 1945. He is now on duty in Tokyo, where Mrs. Dumas and I plan to spend Christmas with him and our new daughter-in-law whom we have not yet had the pleasure of seeing. My own active service ended there, where while serving as a G-I for the occupation, in General MacArthur's headquarters, I was hit at my desk with a coronary occlusion and was eventually returned to an Army hospital in the States and retired.

Recent information on Beta chapter gained from their much appreciated "Altar and Skull" tells of the fire at the fraternity house in 1945 and the loss, among other things, of the box and its contents. That prompts me to send the skull now, with the hope that it may add something of old Davidson tradition to their new domain.

I remember with the keenest of pleasure the years I lived in your home (1913–1916) while I was taking my M.A. and the splendid hospitality of your fine father and mother. You and Adele were then so small that you may not remember it. Nevertheless, it has caused me to retain a real interest in your career and to be proud of your own war service as well as that you are now performing in these days of uneasy peace.

Your performance of this duty for me will cause me to be sincerely grateful, and to hope that I may be able some day to reciprocate the courtesy.

With best wishes, yours in the bonds of pike.

Walter A. Dumas

You will note that the skull itself disproves the story of 'an old Negro man.' We have for years called the skull 'Ichabod' for obvious reasons.

WAD

Through the years, many writers have penned their versions of this as a ghost tale. The following is my rendition of what happened, from the perspective of a young Davidson student who learns the truth about the skull from an old doctor who knows the story firsthand. The doctor begins:

*"It's a terrible secret I've kept all these years. Four of us were involved, but I'm the only one still alive," the old doctor told the young student. "To tell the truth, it's a relief to unburden myself," he continued. "It all started our last year in medical school at Davidson College. We had a rare night out to see a show in nearby Salisbury. From the time we disembarked from the buggy, it was all we heard.*

*"Everyone was talking about the tragic death of a beautiful young woman whose family was prominent in the community. While we were sorry for the family, we didn't know the girl, so we carried on with our revelry. We stopped for supper and drinks after the show, so it was late when we finally started back to Charlotte. The cemetery is on the outskirts of town and as we passed it, an idea occurred to us. We never should have acted on it, but we did.*

*"You have to understand that in those days medical students were responsible for obtaining their own cadavers. This was usually accomplished by some polite and discreet grave robbing. By this I mean that students dug up a grave without anyone being the wiser, especially the*

85

family of the deceased. This seemed a good opportunity to acquire the corpse needed to complete the term. We'd had too much to drink and weren't thinking clearly. The four of us made a hasty decision to dig up the girl's body. We found some shovels in a shed at the edge of the cemetery and used them. I had to break open the latch on the casket but it finally swung open. There she was, all right. Quickly, we wrapped her in a blanket that was in the back of the wagon and then loaded her in the bed of the wagon. We threw the casket and dirt back into the hole and covered it up as fast as we could. After returning the tools to where we had found them, we beat a hasty retreat. No one would have been the wiser if a big rainstorm hadn't taken place early that next morning.

"The storm washed away the topsoil that hadn't been packed back as well as it should have been. The next day when the father and mother went to the cemetery to visit the gravesite, they found a partially exposed casket. Unfortunately, they also found out that it had been broken open and that the corpse was missing. The father went mad! He swore vengeance on the grave robbers who had taken his daughter. A huge hunt was organized, led by the local sheriff.

"Meanwhile, we had arrived back at the college and brought the body to my room. Exhausted from the ordeal, we slept until a commotion woke us up. A fellow med student told us the authorities were at the dean's office demanding to search the school for the missing corpse. The father and authorities were sure med students had taken the body to be used as a cadaver. We knew this meant we would be arrested and subsequently expelled. A couple of us had planned to boil the body in a barrel that was used for that purpose, as soon as we could do it without arousing suspicion. This wouldn't be difficult because the school never asked too many questions as to where the cadavers came from. But now there was no time for that. We had to hide it, and fast.

"There was an entrance to the attic in the farthest corner of the floor our rooms were on. We took the bundle and a lantern and proceeded as quickly as we could down the hall. I climbed up on my buddy's shoulders and pulled on the small hook that was attached to the ceiling. It opened the door that held the stairs to the attic. I yanked as hard as I could, which unfolded them so fast the bottom steps nearly took off my head. We half-ran, half-stumbled up the stairs, awkwardly carrying the wrapped body. There wasn't anything up there. If we just left the body in the attic, it would have been easily discovered. Just as panic was really setting in, we saw that the top of one of the giant hollow columns had come loose. My roommate scrambled back down the tiny opening to get some tools."

"It seemed like forever before he returned. 'They're on their way to search our building next, I just heard!' he breathlessly reported. As if our lives depended on it, and I guess they did, we worked to finish loosening the board. When our efforts were rewarded, we struggled to lift her up over our heads and then dropped her into the opening. With lightning speed we sealed the opening and got out of there. Almost immediately after we finished and got back in our respective rooms, the dean, accompanied by the sheriff and a well-dressed man, knocked on the door. They looked everywhere, from the closet to under the bed. 'Sorry to bother you boys,' the sheriff said apologetically as the men exited our room and headed down the hall. When they finished searching all the rooms and still hadn't found anything, the sheriff asked the dean if there was an attic or basement. The dean slowly nodded. 'This building has a small overhead storage space, but it's never used, so I doubt . . .' The taller, expensively dressed gentleman spoke up. 'Search it, sheriff,' he ordered.

"My heart skipped a beat as I realized we had left the lantern in the attic. The dean led the way to the opening and pulled down the attic steps. Many of us had gathered to watch the activity. 'Get me a lantern,' the dean commanded one of the students. The boy ran to his room and soon returned with one that he handed over to the sheriff. He nodded at the young man and proceeded to climb the narrow steps as best he could. He possessed a large frame that made the task difficult. When the upper part of his body was through the opening, the sheriff held the lantern up high and cautiously swung it from left to right. The big man remained on the steps as he surveyed what the light illuminated. After a few minutes, he descended. 'Nothing there,' he reported.

"The dean was promising there was no way any of his students could have been involved in such a terrible deed. All the while, the well-groomed man was insisting someone from the school was behind the theft. The sheriff wordlessly followed the two men as they left the building and walked across the campus. We held our breaths until they departed."

The old man paused in his story telling as he relit his pipe. He offered me a drink, but I declined. I hoped he wouldn't have one either, since I was anxious for him to get on with the fascinating tale. However, he made himself a drink and took a long sip before settling back into his chair. He took another swallow before setting it down on the table next to him. The doc chuckled as he noticed my agitation. "You're wondering what happened to the body, aren't you?" he asked me. I nodded several times.

"We were afraid to try to remove the corpse for fear of getting caught. After a tense discussion or two on the subject, the four of us never talked about it again. Over the years, students and faculty alike have reported seeing her. I am sure she is the same woman that you have seen," he said as he waved his pipe in my direction.

I gasped in amazement. "How did you know that I've seen her?" I shouted.

"It was obvious by the way you reacted as I told the story, but I already knew. It's no accident that you're here. I asked the dean who was residing in my old room and he told me that it was you. That's why I invited you out this evening."

I thought I had been invited to meet with the doctor because he was getting ready to retire and I was about to graduate. I thought he was looking for an apprentice and was hopeful he was considering me. As I was mentally sorting all this out, the old man watched me intently. "How do you know it's the same girl?" I finally asked. This time he nodded several times and then walked across the room to a desk.

The doc pulled open the second drawer from the bottom and extracted an item I couldn't see. When he handed it to me, I saw it was an exquisite silver locket, suspended on a long silver chain. "This fell off her neck while we were hastily transporting the body and I shoved it in my pocket and forgot all about it for a while."

With trembling fingers, I opened it and found a photo of an exquisite young woman. No doubt—it was her! It was the face that had *haunted me during my entire academic tenure at the college. I told him about when I had first seen her and how I felt when I realized she wasn't real. I also explained how my friends all thought I was crazy until she was seen by a couple of other students. "Finally, we were told about the legend, but all we were told is that the spirit of a lovely young lady shows herself to a few people. No one knows what brought her to the college. It has been driving me crazy. I'm grateful that you shared your story with me, sir."*

*"Well now, I don't believe in secrets between colleagues, do you?" the old doc asked with a sly smile.*

*About the college...*
Davidson College is an institution of higher learning established by the Presbyterians of North Carolina in 1837. The college is named in honor of General William Lee Davidson, a local Revolutionary War hero who died at the battle of Cowan's Ford in 1781. 209 Ridge Road, Davidson, NC 28036.

# TRAGEDY ABOARD THE QUEEN OF SOUNDS

Outer Banks

*Figures were seen moving around on the decks, but witnesses couldn't determine who or what they were. At midnight, a horrific scream was heard just before the ship exploded.*

Corporal Pierre Godette, or "Frenchy" to those who knew him, was stationed at Roanoke Island (Outer Banks) during the Civil War. The young man took to the area like a fish to water. When the war was over, he finessed a government job on the island. Some years later, Godette was forced to find other employment when the government did away with the position. Fun-loving Frenchy had managed to save a fair sum, but it wasn't enough to support him for the rest of his life.

The reveler came up with a creative solution that would keep him gainfully employed without having to leave Roanoke Island. He used his savings to have a showboat built. Powered by a steam engine, the three-level vessel was made with the finest timber and imported furnishings. The main level held the ballroom and bar, which also contained gaming tables. The top deck had promenades and luxurious private rooms. Godette spared no expense. He even had a player piano specially made for his gambling and party boat.

The vessel was christened the *Queen of Sounds*. Many people gathered onshore to wave and watch as the showboat chugged by, and even they could hear the tunes the piano cranked out. The showboat was a success. The *Queen of Sounds* made multiple daily stops at Elizabeth City, Currituck, and Manteo. Performers were hired from as far away as Philadelphia to act in plays. The boat ran during the spring, summer, and fall. In the winter, necessary repairs were made. To most folks, Frenchy seemed to be on top of the world. He was doing what he loved and the boat was making him a great deal of money.

But Godette was drinking too much and it was clouding his judgment. He had always enjoyed whiskey, but now he was consuming much more than he used to. It could have been from boredom, but many believed it was the influence of his new girlfriend. She practiced black magic and got Frenchy heavily involved as well. All the chants, invocations, sorcery, and related mumbo-jumbo deeply confused him and brought out a dark side that he had trouble coping with, so he drank even more.

One summer night, he announced to some patrons that he was going to conjure up the Devil himself to come aboard his boat! What's more, he proposed to do it on a Sunday night. This was considered blasphemy by all who heard his proclamation. Many begged Godette not to go through with his plan. These were God-fearing people and they knew no good could come of it, but there was no talking the man out of the notion.

That Sunday night, the boat was closed to all but Frenchy Godette and his crew. What happened aboard the vessel that night remains a mystery. Area residents said they heard the player piano. Some claimed to have seen Godette standing on the top deck. The ship's lights flickered several times. Figures were seen moving around on the decks, but witnesses couldn't determine who or what they were. At midnight, a horrific scream was heard just before the ship exploded. Those who saw it say there was a flash of light and then the *Queen of Sounds* seemed to come clean out of the water fully intact and burst into thousands of pieces. Afterwards, sulfur could be smelled as far as two miles away.

There were no survivors to tell what happened that night. There are many theories. The most plausible is that the boiler blew up. Some swear the Devil did make an appearance and took Frenchy Godette back with him. Legend has it that if you stand near the bridge that joins Nags Head to Roanoke Island, you can, on rare occasions, see the reflection of mysterious lights on the water. It's believed they belong to the *Queen of Sounds*.

# THE CONFEDERATE SOLDIER AND THE UNKNOWN SPY

Morehead City

*As she paused near the water's edge, taking in a deep breath of cool night air, a large man emerged from the shadows.*

*I*t was a cold, moonless March night. Dampness hung in the air as the fog rolled in across the river. The streets of Morehead City were deserted. It really wasn't a good night to be out, but Emeline Pigott didn't mind. She liked evening strolls when she could be alone with her thoughts. And her thoughts weren't those of an average twenty-two-year-old girl. Emeline was interested in so many things. She longed to know more about the world and hoped to travel to far away places someday. She cared about politics and the war. She wanted to do more than knit blankets and sew clothing for troops. Emeline wanted to make a real difference. And she wouldn't mind a little excitement!

Little did Emeline know that she would get all she wanted that very night. As she paused near the water's edge, taking in a deep breath of cool night air, a large man emerged from the shadows.

"Please don't scream!" he cautioned. "I mean you no harm." As he watched her mouth open as if to scream, he cried out, "I beg you to listen to me. I mean you no harm. I just need you to relay a message."

Slowly she closed her mouth and studied the man. Why he was no man! He wasn't even as old as she was! Realizing that the young man could have already hurt her if he meant to, she asked, "What is this message, that you need to hide in the shadows and then come out to tell the first stranger you encounter?"

"The Federals are going to blow up the Trent River Bridge and seize New Bern within the next twenty-four hours."

Emeline was about to challenge how he could possibly know this when she realized he was wearing a uniform of a Federal officer. "You're a Union soldier!" she exclaimed. "Why should I believe that you wish to help the Confederates?"

"Ma'am, I swear to you on my mama's life that I am surely serious. I have family in New Bern and I don't wish to see them harmed. I don't know the exact time we'll attack, but we'll come ashore at the mouth of Slocum's Creek." Without another word, the young officer disappeared back into the shadows.

Emeline sank down onto a big piece of driftwood. She sat lost in thought for several minutes. If she believed what she had been told, she must do something about it. But what if it was some kind of trap? Her father was a Confederate sympathizer. They sometimes hid Rebel soldiers in their cellar. What if someone had gotten suspicious and was testing the Pigott family loyalty? She could be putting not just herself in jeopardy, but her family as well. Still, what if it the young man had been telling the truth? She would be putting the whole town and all their troops in great danger by ignoring the warning.

Emeline made up her mind. She didn't believe the fellow was lying. She had good instincts and they told her that he was telling the truth. She had better let someone know soon! Emeline ran all the way home. Upon reaching the property, she headed directly to the stable. Emeline saddled her horse as quickly and quietly as possible. She must tell no one of her mission and if she were caught it would be impossible to explain why she was slipping out into the late night on horseback. It took longer than she had hoped, since she didn't normally saddle her own horse, but she didn't dare rouse the stable boy.

Emeline had been on the road to New Bern for some time when a voice called out, "Halt!" A Confederate sentry came out of the bushes alongside the road and grabbed the reins of her horse.

"I beg your pardon! Kindly let go of my horse!" she demanded.

"Where are you heading, ma'am?" he asked, still controlling her horse.

"To speak with your commanding officer," Emeline answered.

The young man was clearly startled by her announcement. As he glanced up, he noticed her clothing. She was in a dress complete with a fitted bodice, fancy boots, and a very expensive-looking cloak.

"Now what business would you have with my captain?" he asked with a wry grin.

"Not your captain. I must talk to your colonel. I don't have all night so if you'll kindly let me be on my way, and perhaps tell me how much farther it is, I'd greatly appreciate that," Emeline said.

The sentry was really confused by now. He didn't know what she was up to but he figured she must have good reason for undertaking such a dangerous task. "You'll see a trail off to the left 'bout eight miles up. Stay on the trail and you'll get there."

Emeline thanked him and then gently kicked her horse to get him moving. She found the trail without difficulty and wondered how much farther it would be when another Confederate soldier approached her. Emeline pleaded with him that she must speak to Colonel Taylor immediately.

"I'm sorry, ma'am. That's not possible. Colonel Taylor's too busy for visitors."

"I have vital information that I must share with him. Please!"

Again her persuasive powers prevailed. They soon reached the camp, where she was finally able to speak with Colonel Taylor. Even though her heart was beating wildly, she kept her head and calmly explained her purpose. The colonel was most impressed with this charming young lady. Not many women would have had the nerve to do what she had done. Given her sweet looks, she would not be suspected of being a spy.

"You have been very brave, my dear. I truly commend you on your efforts tonight. You may also be of further service, if you would be so inclined."

"How?" she asked.

"If you happened to hear anything that might help us and you would be willing to get the information to me, it would be a great aid to our efforts."

"You want me to be a spy for the Confederates?" Emeline asked.

"I wouldn't want you to go to any extraordinary measures, just if you heard talk and could pass along what you heard . . . " he broke off. "Never mind. It could be dangerous and I couldn't ask you to put yourself in that position."

"I'll do it! I want to help and I think that I can," Emeline announced.

"You do know that if you get caught trying to pass a message, you will most likely be hanged. You need to think carefully before deciding. This is no game. You'll be hanged the same as any man if you're caught," the colonel warned.

She promised she was up for it and that she would be very careful. It was arranged for her to pass along any news through a loyal friend of the family who was also a rebel sympathizer. Captain McRae was assigned to escort Ms. Pigott as close to Morehead City as he dared.

Emeline woke to the sound of cannon fire on the morning of March 13, 1862. Union forces attacked at Slocum's Creek. Despite the advance warning, the Confederates could not defeat them. New Bern and Morehead City had fallen to the enemy! The shrewd young lady knew that the next attack would be on Fort Macon—but when? The war would surely be over if the General Burnside and his men were to take Fort Macon.

Emeline got the answer she needed the following night at a party. Many Union soldiers were in attendance, including an officer who was obviously smitten with her. Using this to her advantage, she asked if he would like to accompany her to a party. Major Allen replied that he would be happy to do so, provided the party wasn't held on the twenty-third. She used a hairpiece to conceal the secret message. When she had opportunity, she slid the little slip of paper from its hiding spot and gave it to her contact.

These rendezvous occurred a few times, as did meetings with Captain Stokes McRae. The officer came to her home in disguise on several occasions. These were social get togethers, not related to the war. They had grown to deeply enjoy each other's company, even though it could be dangerous for both of them if anyone discovered his true identity. Within a few months, he asked her to marry him after the war. It remained a secret engagement.

During February 1865, Emeline was on her way to deliver a message when two Union soldiers approached her. They accused her of spying and demanded that she accompany them. On the way to the prison, she managed to slide the paper out of her hair and slip it into her mouth. Emeline quickly swallowed the evidence. She was searched as soon as she arrived at the prison. A woman conducted a thorough search but no incriminating message was found. She was questioned at length but the questioning revealed nothing. No evidence could be produced. Still, the officer refused to release Emeline.

She remained a prisoner until an attempt was made on her life one night. She realized that they didn't care about proof, they were sure she was a spy and so they were going to get rid of her—one way or another. Emeline demanded to see a high-ranking Union soldier who she knew had also been helping the Confederates.

"If you don't get me out of this place by nightfall, you're going to be sharing these quarters with me," Emeline promised. "At least until your execution date!"

It was nearly suppertime when a guard opened the door to her cell and led her outside to where her father waited. Emeline Pigott was free once again. Her spying days were over. In fact, the war ended a few months later. General Lee surrendered and Emeline waited for her fiancé to come home. A fellow Confederate officer brought the news that Captain McRae had died in battle, back in Gettysburg. He brought the corpse so that his friend could have a proper burial. It was hard to know for sure if the right body had been recovered.

Emeline buried him in the family cemetery with a simple tombstone, Unknown Soldier. Upon her death, she was buried next to the Unknown Soldier. On certain nights when the fog rolls in from the river and the moonlight is faint, the spirits of Emeline Pigott and Stokes McRae have been seen walking along Arendell road or down by the river. He is dressed in gray, presumably a Confederate uniform, and she is wearing a pretty dress and fancy cloak.

*About the Civil War . . .*

North Carolina was the last of the Southern states to secede, yet it sent more troops and supplies and suffered more losses than any other Southern state. Approximately 40,000 North Carolinians were killed during the war.

# GHOST SHIP OF DIAMOND SHOALS

Outer Banks

*They could get only within a quarter mile of the ship, due to the high surf and rough swells. The men circled it several times, calling out for a response from someone aboard, but the rescuers received no answer.*

I n years past, mariners dreaded navigating the waters surrounding North Carolina's Outer Banks, a succession of skinny islands stretching roughly 175 miles from Virginia southward to Cape Lookout. They dubbed the area "Graveyard of the Atlantic" because over six hundred ships had sunk there. Mariners relied heavily on lighthouse keepers, lifesaving stations, and the Coast Guard crew to keep them afloat or rescue them when the sea tried to take them. These men knew that how well they performed their duties meant the difference between life and death.

When the crew at the Hattcras Inlet Coast Guard Station was awakened by an alarm on January 31, 1921, they moved quickly and efficiently. The surfman on lookout duty had alerted them to a ship in distress he had spotted. The lookouts at Big Kinnakeet, Creeds Hill, and Cape Hatteras Coast Guard Stations also noted the ship off in the distance. Men representing all four stations were sent in two rescue boats. The huge, five-masted schooner appeared to be stuck on the outer tip of Diamond Shoals, and was slowly sinking.

The rescuers noted that no distress signal had been given and that there weren't any signs of life aboard the vessel. They could get only within a quarter mile of the ship, due to the high surf and rough swells. The men circled it several times, calling out for a response from someone aboard, but the rescuers received no answer. Finally the men returned to the station and sent in the report. A quick investigation revealed that the ship was the *Carroll A. Deering*, first launched in Maine on April 4, 1919. *Carroll A. Deering*, named after the owner's son, was the last schooner ever built.

The owner, G.G. Deering Company, was notified, and it authorized the Coast Guard to go aboard and find out what was wrong. Coast Guard cutters *Seminole* (stationed in Wilmington, North Carolina) and *Manning* (stationed in Norfolk, Virginia) as well as the wrecking tug *Rescue* (stationed in Norfolk, Virginia) were dispatched to the shipwreck, but it was four days before the men were able to board because of the bad weather. The ship had suffered quite a bit of damage during that time. Once the officials were able to search the ship, they made some eerie discoveries.

Everything seemed to be in place except some key items. The ship's log and navigational instruments were missing. Nothing seemed to indicate that there had been a problem or reason for a quick departure, except that dinner had been served in the dining hall and it didn't look like anything had been eaten. Cooking pots remained on the stove of the galley, but the fire that kept the food warm had long expired. Everything was cold to the touch. The only living thing the search party found was a cat.

Someone called out that the yawl boat (lifeboat) was missing, and all the men scrambled up to the top deck. They discovered that the anchors were also missing. The cables that connected the steering wheel to the rudder had been cut. It would have taken an ax to cut through the thick rope cables. Why would anyone do that? There was also a gash on the outside of the ship near where the ladder had been positioned.

The continuous beating the vessel was taking from the combination of the wind and the pounding waves was driving the ship aground at a rapid rate. The rescuers scooped up the gray cat and made a hasty retreat. When the ship's condition and the strange circumstances were reported to Coast Guard headquarters, a major search was initiated all along the coast. Every inch of water, including tiny bays and inlets, was searched. No further wreckage of any kind was discovered. Despite an investigation that lasted many days, nothing else from the ship was ever found. No one known to be aboard the *Carroll A. Deering*, which has been nicknamed the ghost ship, was ever heard from again.

Captain F. Merritt, a World War I hero with a citation for bravery, had been carefully chosen to command the schooner. However, he became ill at Delaware Breakwater and was replaced by Captain W. M. Wormell of Portland, Maine. It was eventually discovered that

Captain Merritt had gotten very sick en route from Newport News to Rio de Janeiro. He had put in at Lewes, Delaware, and was taken to a hospital. Captain W.M. Wormell was brought aboard to assume Captain Merritt's duties. The vessel delivered its cargo of coal to Rio de Janeiro and then sailed on to Barbados. Upon arrival, the captain learned there was no cargo to pick up at Barbados. The ship was to return to Newport News. The investigation proved that the *Carroll A. Deering* left Bridgetown, a port in Barbados, on January 9, 1921.

Aboard were the captain, the first mate, and eight members of the crew. A friend or acquaintance of Captain Wormell gave testimony during the investigation that the skipper had told him he anticipated trouble. Wormell also told him that his first mate, Officer McClellan, was no good. While in port, the crew got rip-roaring drunk and McClellan was arrested, but the captain arranged his release and they set out.

*Carroll A. Deering* was logged as passing the Cape Fear Lightship, which was positioned at Wilmington, on January 23, 1921. No problems or oddities were noted. Six nights later the Cape Lookout Lightship sighted the ship. It is strange that it would have taken the vessel six days to travel just seventy miles north.

A strange conversation occurred between the watch officer of the Cape Lookout Lightship and someone on the *Carroll A. Deering*. Someone aboard the *Carroll A. Deering* shouted through a megaphone that the captain had requested other ships steer clear of the vessel because she had lost her anchors during a storm. The lightship tender thought this was odd because no storms had been reported. Members of the crew were spotted on deck, although they didn't appear to be busy. The ship seemed to be making good time, yet nothing more was seen or heard of the *Carroll A. Deering* until the Hatteras Coast Guard spotted the foundering ship on January 31, 1921.

As if this was not enough of a mystery, it was discovered that a passenger boarded in South America. However, the investigation didn't uncover the name of the secret passenger. The ship was only permitted to carry ten men, as per its registration under U.S. maritime regulations, so that probably explains why the eleventh passenger wasn't documented.

The shipwreck was added to navigational charts as a possible hazard to mariners. Despite the best efforts of the U.S. Navy, the Justice Department, and the Commerce Department, what happened was not discovered. Many speculated it must have had something to do with piracy, but there were no signs of an altercation and the ship's captain appeared to be above reproach. His daughter, Miss Wormell, took part in the investigation. Above all, she didn't want her father's name forever linked to piracy or negligence.

A break in the mystery came one day when a bottle with a message washed ashore at Cape Hatteras and was found by a local resident. The note said that pirates had attacked the *Carroll A. Deering*, and those who survived the attack were put into lifeboats without oars or provisions. The government investigated the note, despite the fact that they considered it ludicrous that pirates would seize a ship at Hatteras in 1921. The inquiry resulted in a confession by the man who wrote the note, put it in a bottle, and then claimed to have found it on the shore.

In the end, the government concluded that the crew left the sinking ship on a lifeboat and must have been lost at sea while trying to escape. That sounds plausible except that no trace of the yawl or the men was ever found; not even a lifejacket or an article of clothing or a piece of the boat—nothing. Miss Wormell still contends that the crew encountered foul play, although there is no evidence to support that claim. Ultimately, the government stopped looking for answers.

The owners of the sunken ship hired Merritt Chapman Wrecking Corporation to salvage some of the items, which were sold at an auction. Later, a nor'easter scattered the remaining hulk all over the shoreline. Locals grabbed up usable wreckage. Remnants from the shipwreck helped build many houses along the Outer Banks. The stern sank and is part of the Graveyard of the Atlantic. The Coast Guard used explosives to blow up the remaining wreckage to keep it from being a navigational hazard.

Although the physical evidence of the mysterious ship is long gone, legend has it that strange sounds are sometimes heard when bad nor'easter storms blow through Hatteras in February. Some say it's just the wind, but others believe it may be the spirits of the crew of the *Carroll A. Deering* trying to tell us what happened to them.

It's worth mentioning that around the same time as the *Carroll A. Deering* incident, the steamer *Hewitt* disappeared without a trace along the Atlantic Coast. Some believe Russian pirates took both vessels. Author Edward Rowe Snow included this possibility in his publication, *Mysteries and Adventures Along the Atlantic Coast*: "When this theory was investigated, it was proved that the American representative of the *Washington Post* knew of several vessels entering the port of Vladivostok under the command of Russian crews. The names of the ships in every case had been obliterated. Eight ships had disappeared at the same time that the *Deering* was wrecked, including the *Entine, Florina, Svartskag, Lorringa* and *Hewitt*. The romantic solution is that 20th Century pirates captured and killed the crew with intention of taking the ship, which in the meantime foundered on the Outer Diamond. What happened to the *Carroll A. Deering* is considered by many to be the greatest mystery of the seas during the first half of the 20th Century."

See page 144 for a Coast Guard report on the *Deering*.

*Worth visiting . . .*
The Graveyard of the Atlantic Museum is the world's only museum devoted solely to the shipwrecks and maritime history of the Outer Banks. This 19,000-square-foot-museum and gift shop at the Hatteras–Ocracoke Ferry Terminal and U.S. Coast Guard Base houses paraphernalia from more than 1,000 ships wrecked along North Carolina's coast, including the *Carroll A. Deering*. The structure was built to withstand most hurricanes. The engineers were sure that they had outsmarted Mother Nature. But a few years ago, a hurricane blew through and separated Hatteras Island from the mainland, making it impossible to visit the museum until the new inlet was filled in by the Army Corp of Engineers. A lesson from Mother

Nature! For more information call (252) 986-2995 or visit www. graveyardoftheatlantic.com.

The Chicamacomico Lifesaving Station Historic Site (pronounced chik-a-ma-COM-i-co) was one of the first of many stations placed along the Outer Banks. This station and its outbuildings are considered to be one of the most complete U.S. Lifesaving Service/ Coast Guard Station complexes on the Atlantic Coast. The original building, constructed in 1874, was turned into a boathouse when the new shingle-style station was built in 1911. Part of the 30,318 acres that comprise Cape Hatteras National Seashore, the Chicamacomico Station is located on NC 12 in Rodanthe, about twenty-five miles south of Nags Head at the 39.5 milepost. For more information, call (252) 987-1552 or visit www.chicamacomico.net.

Author's note:
The following four stories
were winners in a statewide
ghost story contest.

# GENTLE SPIRIT

## Dillsboro

Contributed by Elizabeth W. Blythe, Greensboro

*A bit surprised by my question, she first hesitated but then told us that there had been similar incidents reported through the years.*

Nestled in the western part of North Carolina is the tiny town of Dillsboro. It boasts the Jarrett House, an old hotel that serves wonderful home-cooked meals and rents a few rooms to overnight guests.

Several years ago, my husband and I decided to spend the night there. We enjoyed a delicious meal and the place's quaint atmosphere. A pleasant breeze enveloped us as we sat in rocking chairs on the front porch, the perfect ending to a very busy day.

Our room on the second floor had the look of a bygone era, with oversized antique furnishings and fluttering lace curtains. Positioned away from each other were two beds, double and single.

We went to sleep in the double bed. But well into the night, I awakened abruptly. Someone was touching my head. Then I felt a hand on my brow. With a very gentle touch, it patted my bangs and the top of my head again. Thinking it was my husband, I turned over to respond, but he wasn't next to me. Startled, I looked around the dimly lit room and saw him sound asleep in the single bed next to the bathroom.

After waking him, we talked. He explained that he had gotten restless during the night and decided to sleep in the other bed so I would not be disturbed.

Next morning at breakfast I decided to ask our waiter if the hotel was haunted. He said he had only worked there a short time, but he would ask some of the kitchen help about it. He returned to tell us that there had been reports, but the staff was told not to discuss it, especially with guests. Then the waiter requested we not divulge his comments regarding the matter.

However, as we checked out of the hotel that morning, I decided to ask the cashier if any unusual happenings had ever occurred there. A bit surprised by my question, she first hesitated but then told us that there had been similar incidents reported through the years. She also said that some of the housekeeping staff had, at various times, sensed something unusual, particularly on the second floor, and it was thought to be a presence—that of a lady, perhaps.

The rumor is, the cashier said, that folks thought the presence might be Mrs. Jarrett, who had a reputation for tucking her children in at bedtime and caressing them gently, especially if they were ill.

# Pot of Gold

## Elk Park

Contributed by Rob Kincaid, Greensboro

*In the morning, his curiosity still at a peak, Bobby persuaded his father to go with him into the woods to find the strangers.*

$F$or many years, my grandmother has told me the story of her cousin, who was frightened beyond belief by "haints" he stumbled upon in the woods on a dark mountain night in rural North Carolina. The following is my recollection of that story.

Cousin Bobby Turbyfield was a young man who lived on the banks of the Elk River in eastern Avery County. He was, by all accounts, normal, with a fondness for the moving picture shows in town.

Mountain life was hard, filled with work and very little else. Farm boys were used to breaking a sweat well before the sun came up. Mountain life was also dull, and a young man of twenty needed an outlet. In the town of Elk Park, that outlet was the fifty-seat movie theater beside Brinkley's Hardware.

Bobby was fully versed in the trouble a boy could encounter after dark. His parents and older relatives had brought him up with the understanding that "no good could come to a body adder dark" and every attempt should be made to get back home. In the mountains, darkness falls like a thick, dark, woolen blanket and at the time was accentuated by the lack of electric lighting. There was very little to break the blackness.

One cool Friday night in late October, Bobby headed home after dark from the movie theater. He took a shortcut through the woods, a well-worn path dense with low-growing brush and still-leafy trees—a path he had walked many times in an effort to shorten the three-mile journey home. Bobby's stride kept pace with his fast-beating heart.

As he came over a small hill and headed down into a valley, he saw what appeared to be a light glowing in the distance. As he approached what he assumed would be local campers, he slowed his rapid pace to a less noisy, step-by-single-step progression.

When he got a clear view of the scene, he stopped cold. Two people, a man and woman, dressed in simple black and white clothes and surrounded by a heavy, cool mist, stood in the light. The man wore a black hat, full coat, knee britches, white knee socks, and black shoes with bright buckles. The woman wore a black, full-length dress, white cotton shirt, and a large bonnet that partially obscured her face. The dim yellow light coming from a lantern hanging in a nearby tree cast their faces in deep shadows, making them look old and wrinkled. They definitely weren't from around those parts.

As he watched the ghostlike figures, his idea of walking closer and speaking to them quickly changed. They carefully moved an old black iron pot that apparently was very heavy. The pot had come out of a huge hole surrounded by dead grass, making Bobby think a wagon-size boulder nearby had been covering its hiding place. While he stood there in frightened silence, the two figures maneuvered the pot to a spot close by and set it down. As they did so, its contents came into clear view: gold coins filled the pot to the brim.

The sight of the coins, given the hard times of the region, made Bobby even uneasier. What had he stumbled onto? Would the people he was spying on appreciate his knowledge of their actions? Silently, he climbed back up the hill and headed home in another direction.

He could hardly contain his fear and amazement. Who were these people, and how had they moved a boulder the size of a wagon? Why were they dressed as they were, and where had all that gold come from?

When he got home, he told his parents what he'd seen and nearly collapsed from exhaustion and fright. But his parents were skeptical of the story and figured it was an excuse for being late.

In the morning, his curiosity still at a peak, Bobby persuaded his father to go with him into the woods to find the strangers. A heavy pot like the one they were moving would be difficult to handle and should have kept them in the area past dawn, he reasoned.

As Bobby and his father walked, Bobby started to feel both excitement and fright at the idea of a face-to-face encounter with the two mysterious people and their gold. He and his father slowed their pace as they neared the site to avoid making noise.

To the surprise and disappointment of both father and son, the pilgrims were gone, along with the pot and its contents. What was left, however, was a hole in the ground and a clear mark that the pot had made. The grass around that spot was pale and lifeless, like that found under large objects.

The story of this late-night encounter and the impression of the pot that had been left in the ground would dazzle the local residents for years to come. The spot remained visible for many years, drawing curious visitors.

My grandmother told this story to my brother and me, telling us to stay within sight at all times and get home before dark. She had no explanation for this event but said she had seen the giant rock that had been moved and the mark the pot had made in the ground.

The mountain folk decided that Bobby had stumbled upon the ghosts of early settlers who had gotten lost on the long, perilous journey out west. After they met with some unknown fate, they returned from the afterlife to retrieve their savings, buried forever in the wilderness of the North Carolina mountains.

# THE SHADOW MAN

Big Lick

Contributed by Richard Morton, Oakboro

*I wasn't scared as much as fascinated, but Donna started screaming and I took off just to settle her nerves.*

*I* have had one experience that I classify as a ghost story, for lack of any other explanation. This incident happened in September 1969 in Stanly County, near the community of Big Lick. At the time, Big Lick was nothing more than a crossroads with a gas station on one corner. I was a junior at UNC Charlotte, majoring in civil engineering, and I was living at home with my parents, James and Imogene Morton.

One evening, my girlfriend, Gail Smith, and her friend Donna Lowder dropped by to see me. This was unusual because we usually called each other every day but did not see each other during the week since she lived in Albemarle. They arrived late in the day, maybe at 6:30 or so, and it was nearly dark.

Because my parents' house is small and they were both home, we decided to ride around a little while in Gail's Corvair. As the darkness grew, I decided to try and spook Gail and Donna a little by driving down the dirt road in front of my parents' house. The road is maybe two miles long and had only three houses then. There is a long, deserted stretch where the road descends down a hill to a small creek, crossed by a little one-lane bridge without side rails, then rises steeply. I had always heard as a child that someone had committed suicide near this bridge years before, but I didn't really know any of the specifics.

As we neared the bridge, I started slowing down, preparing to tell them this story. By this time it was dark, and I had the headlights on. As we neared the bridge I could see what I thought was a man walking up the hill on the other side. He looked like a shadow man, as he had no real substance and you could see through him, but was still recognizable as a person.

Donna and I were looking at this thing, but Gail was looking

115

down, fiddling with the cigarette lighter. I had just started to say, "What the heck is that?," when all of a sudden as if he realized we were watching, the shadow man condensed into a ball of white light about the size of a basketball. I was hoping it would hover awhile so we could observe it, but it shot off to our left. Only two or three seconds had elapsed from the time I spotted the man until he disappeared.

I wasn't scared as much as fascinated, but Donna started screaming and I took off just to settle her nerves. Gail missed the whole thing and was wondering what in the world was going on. Donna was really upset, so we went back home and related the story to my parents. Donna's frightened demeanor made my parents believe us, but there really wasn't much they could do other than listen. It made the hair stand up on the back of your neck— you know you're looking at something that is not explainable in our cause-and-effect world.

I've been down that same road other times at night but have never seen anything strange again and have never heard anyone else report anything. The area looks pretty much the same now as it did then, but there is a subdivision going up nearby, and the state is going to pave the road soon. Without Donna's reaction, I might have tried to explain it away, but I know what I saw, and her description was identical to mine.

# *B*LACKBEARD'S TALE

### Pamlico Sound

Contributed by Robert F. Bell, Ridgeway, VA

(This is a story about the author's ancestors,
written for his grandchildren.)

*"Who are you, sir, and where do you come from?"—To which the dark intruder snarled, "My name is Thatch, and I come straight from Hell; and I shall soon take you thence if you don't fetch me some brandy."*

*T*here are quiet times along the Pamlico Sound of North Carolina when the breeze is southerly, the night skies are dark, and the fishing boats are in port. Sound travels far across the water, and some say there is a persistent noise that can be heard only from three to four in the morning. The haunting sound is of oars "thunking" in wooden locks and of an angry wail for vengeance. Legend reports the sighting of a ghostlike figure standing astern a small wooden longboat while gaunt sailors row up and down the northern shore of Pamlico Sound from Swan Quarter to Bath. I have seen the vision and heard the cry on more than one occasion, and I was close enough once to make out the call. In an Elizabethan cockney accent, the tall, grizzled specter shouts out the name "Bell" and waves a mighty arm as if inviting us all to face his furious vengeance.

The Colonial Records of North Carolina are clear about the facts of the infamous pirate Blackbeard's death on Ocracoke Island in 1718; and the Virginia Colonial Records concur and even shed further light on the occasions leading up to that fateful battle. Blackbeard had a large and comfortable home in Bath, right next door to the residence of Governor Hyde. He was thought of as a patriot and, at worst, a privateer, but he wholesaled much of his ill-gotten goods to the merchants of the area and entertained widely. Somehow, Edward Thatch, alias Edward Teach, alias Blackbeard the Pirate, had gained tolerance (if not respectability) in Bath despite his heinous behavior at sea and his horrific appearance and evil glare.

Legend has it that Blackbeard sought the hand of Hyde's beautiful daughter in marriage, but she spurned his offer, claiming to love another gentleman. That unfortunate young gentleman promptly disappeared and was never seen again, except that his severed hands were sent in a package to the beautiful daughter of Governor Hyde.

The major player in the demise of Blackbeard was our forefather William Bell, a respected merchant and treasurer of Currituck, precinct of Hyde County. His family were early settlers inland at Bell Bay, about fifteen miles east of Bath. He had a loving wife and one young son, William Jr., whom he worshipped. In those days, there were no roads, and the only means of transportation was by boat. William Bell sold and traded his goods to other planters and settlers up and down Pamlico Sound from his wide, flat-bottomed sailboat (called a piragua).

On the night of September 14, 1717, William Bell was tied up at Chester's Landing, a few miles west of Bell Bay. Within the small cabin of their piragua were Bell, his young son, William Jr., and a young Indian companion. They were on their usual trading route circuit. Sometime between the hours of three and four o'clock that morning, they were stirred by the sound of an approaching longboat and boisterous laughter from the oarsmen. When the tall and swarthy skipper of the longboat stepped aboard Bell's piragua, he shouted for a drink of brandy. Still groggy from sleep, William Bell demanded,

"Who are you, sir, and where do you come from?" To which the dark intruder snarled, "My name is Thatch, and I come straight from Hell; and I shall soon take you thence if you don't fetch me some brandy."

It was Blackbeard himself, no doubt about it—drunk and in a very black mood. An argument ensued and Blackbeard called to his crew for his sword. The argument turned violent. Blackbeard's sword was broken in the fray, and Bell was beaten severely. Their piragua was towed out into the Sound, stripped of all its goods and cash, and set adrift without sails or oars. The longboat was rowed west with the loot, which included sixty-six pounds sterling and a few shillings, and half a keg of coveted brandy. Curiously, Blackbeard also stole a prized family possession: a small, silver cup, uniquely made.

Later that morning, Bell, his son, and the Indian lad were able to make it to shore. William set about ending the career of Blackbeard, whatever it took. He wrote to Alexander Spotswood, who was lieutenant governor of Virginia, and asked for help. He also gave specific information on where Blackbeard's ship, *Adventure*, was located. William did not request help from North Carolina Governor Hyde because it was common knowledge that Blackbeard was paying Hyde handsomely for amnesty and protection.

Spotswood was delighted with the request. The wealthy merchants of Virginia, constantly harassed and robbed by Blackbeard, had demanded action from the Crown. At last, he had a request to tread on the sovereign territory of North Carolina for the worthy cause of justice.

The lieutenant governor dispatched Lt. Robert Maynard and two sloops with orders to arrest or kill Blackbeard and his men. Bell's directions were given to Maynard, and upon arrival at Ocracoke Island (where Blackbeard was hiding) on November 22, 1718, he found the *Adventure* at anchor, as expected, at Teach's Hole, the only deep-water anchorage on the southwestern corner of the island. A fierce battle ensued and resulted in hand-to-hand combat with swords. Blackbeard was a giant of a figure, some say seven feet tall, with long black hair over much of his body. He roared with anger and fought savagely but in the end was felled with over a hundred saber cuts. The few remaining crew were captured and taken to Williamsburg, Virginia, to be tried for piracy.

Maynard severed Blackbeard's head and threw the body overboard. Legend has it that the body of Blackbeard continued thrashing, even without a head, and swam around Maynard's ship three times before sinking to the bottom of Teach's Hole. The grizzled head was affixed to the end of the bowsprit of Maynard's ship for all to see as they set sail back to Virginia.

And among the curiosities found aboard Blackbeard's ship was a unique silver cup that could only have been that of William Bell. There are also many unanswered questions. Bell probably had a history of trading with Blackbeard and his men. All of the other merchants of Pamlico Sound did, and there is no reason to think that Bell had not also profited richly in this trade with the infamous pirate. Bell even knew the precise location of the *Adventure*. Why then was Bell the one to blow the whistle? Was it just a matter of reaching the limit of tolerance for intimidation and bullying? Was this the time when something had to be done? Or were there other, more sinister motives?

Bell was a respected citizen, and Blackbeard certainly needed a cohort with whom he felt he could entrust his booty. We must remember that no one has ever found the very extensive loot of gold, silver, and jewels that Blackbeard amassed during his years of piracy. Although Blackbeard favored the luxury of the town of Bath, with its comfortable homes, it was unlikely he would hide his loot near his domicile. His anchorage was off Ocracoke Island, and he would have had to sail his longboats right past Bell Bay before the approach to Bath. What if he made regular deposits with his then-trusted friend, William Bell, before proceeding on to the respectable Bath? Would simple greed not explain why Bell was anxious to see a fatal end to Blackbeard?

Knowing Blackbeard would never be taken alive, and knowing that Spotswood of Virginia was the only person who could complete the necessary tasks, Bell could have cunningly plotted the embezzlement of Blackbeard's millions. Could the untold millions still be buried somewhere within the hundreds of acres of land surrounding Bell Bay?

We can imagine the fury and anger that possessed Blackbeard when he realized the identity and treachery of his betrayer, and how he cursed the name of our beloved forefather and all his progeny.

Perhaps, that would also explain reports that the head of Blackbeard, affixed to the bowsprit of Maynard's ship, silently mouthed one word over and over: "Bell . . . Bell . . . Bell."

It would also explain why to this day we, the Bells, experience the specter of a seven-foot-tall image standing astern an ancient longboat as it is rowed along the shoreline of Pamlico Sound, and why we alone can hear the wailing and wrathful challenge to our family during the hours of three or four A.M. on very dark and quiet nights in these backwaters of eastern North Carolina.

# STRANGE HAPPENINGS

*Across our state, strange and inexplicable things have taken place (and some are ongoing) that make even the harshest critics of the supernatural scratch their heads desperately seeking rational explanations. While some may label these events as phenomena rather than ghostly occurrences, I would beg to differ. Something that cannot be scientifically explained leaves little other explanation than supernatural, making these phenomena right at home among ghostly tales. Here are a few of my favorite Carolina phenomenona that continue to intrigue, baffle, and unnerve us.*

# CAPE FEAR BOOM

Cape Fear coast

*Long-time residents have found their own answers to this strange phenomenon. They call it the "Seneca Guns."*

*F*rom time to time, noises most commonly described as "booming" are heard along the Cape Fear coast. Residents scramble to take cover, fearing an earthquake. The National Weather Service and National Earthquake Information Center both receive numerous phone calls when the noises are heard. Despite the fact that homes and businesses shake like they would during an earthquake, the National Earthquake Information Center has shown no major earth movement in the Wilmington area. Representatives at the U.S. Geological Survey office also swear there has been no seismic activity in the area when these booms are reported.

When the Cape Fear Boom last happened, just a few months ago, a Belville resident, Curtis Reeves, was sure there must have been an explosion at Military Ocean Terminal at Sunny Point, near Southport. However, military officials stated there had been no problems with the ammunitions depot or anywhere else on the base. A local National Weather Service meteorologist, Ron Steve, in Wilmington swore that whatever occurred was not weather related.

Long-time residents have found their own answers to this strange phenomenon. They call it the "Seneca Guns." Legend has it that the Seneca Indians, who were run off their land by European settlers, have come back for revenge. The story goes that the Indians are shooting powerful guns they got from the same men who took their land. The battle noises are usually heard in late fall and early winter.

A crew member working on a Warner Brothers show that is

**Did you know . . .**

In some parts of ancient Europe, when a new cemetery was completed it was customary to bury a person alive in the first grave so that a ghostly guardian, Ankou (also called "The Graveyard Watcher"),
was created. The idea was that this tormented soul
would frighten off unwanted intruders and spirits so
that the dead would not be disturbed. Yikes!

filmed in Wilmington is certain there is no other explanation. Tim
McKinney, who says that an incident during fall 2005 was the worst
he has experienced, swears the origin lies with the Seneca Indians
and the legend of the Seneca Guns.

More scientific theories include: jets breaking the sound barrier
as part of military exercises at nearby Cherry Point Marine Corps Air
Station in Havelock, a patch of air suddenly becoming hotter than
the air surrounding it and subsequently exploding like a balloon, or
the shifting of the continental shelf. Like most theories that attempt
to explain away the unexplainable, each has significant flaws that
lead us to still question what causes the Cape Fear Boom—modern
man or ancient Indians?

# DEVIL'S STOMPING GROUND
## Siler City

*Several people claim to have seen a pair of red, glowing eyes as they passed the road where the circle lies just beyond.*

One hundred feet off a country road in Siler City, which comprises a small part of Chatham County, lies a patch of grass that most sensible folks steer clear of. The harmless looking turf of grass is a perfect circle, roughly two feet wide and fifteen feet in diameter. So what's the big deal?

It is reported that no one can successfully drive his or her car over the circle. One man who attempted to disprove this said his car stalled and wouldn't restart. He said the same thing happened when he tried with another car on another night.

Animals have the good sense to stay away from the area. Knowledgeable drivers lock their car doors and speed by the spot. Several people claim to have seen a pair of red, glowing eyes as they passed the road where the circle lies just beyond.

Some accounts claim that no one has ever spent the night at the Devil's Stomping Ground. Others say campers have attempted it, but always found themselves well outside of the circle when they awoke.

Ethan Feinsilver, a newspaper journalist, decided to see for himself in October 1998. Trying to laugh off the strange accounts as he set up camp with his two big dogs, the reporter admits his imagination was in full gear. However, Feinsilver successfully spent the night inside the circle. The only disturbing thing that occurred during that long evening was the sound of footfalls.

"They weren't loud enough to be someone walking around the

tent. They were muffled—sort of ghostly," says Feinsilver. Despite getting a full night's sleep—well, at least a full night's stay—at the Devil's Stomping Ground, the journalist cannot be made to deny the existence of something sinister at this site.

# INEXPLICABLE LIGHTS
## Vander and Momeyer

*The switchman was run over by the passing train and his head was chopped off when his body was pulled under the car.*

W e've all heard the stories of headless men carrying a lantern along railroad tracks looking for their missing head. I wrote about the "Mysterious Light at Maco Station" in *Ghosts of the Carolina Coasts*. I wrote about the Pactolus Light in *Ghosts and Legends of the Carolina Coasts*. Now I've found two more train ghosts in Vander (Cumberland County, near Fayetteville) and Momeyer (Nash County, near Rocky Mount).

One could dismiss these lights as urban legend, but there is just enough compelling evidence to reject this assumption. Many credible witnesses have seen them, including newspaper reporters, local authorities, and even President Cleveland when the train stopped at Maco to refuel in 1889.

More importantly, these lights have been investigated by many experts over the years, including a team from the Smithsonian Institute, the Army Corps of Engineers, and a professional ghost hunter and leading authority on ghosts, Hans Holzer.

The story starts out with a switchman smoking a cigarette. He was on the train's platform in the town of Vander when he saw

another train off in the distance coming straight at the standstill train. The man dropped his cigarette and quickly tried to change tracks to divert the approaching train. The engineer also saw the imminent peril and sounded the train's whistle, again and again. It was raining hard and the warning whistle must have been drowned out. By the time the conductor of the other train noticed there was another train on the same tracks, it was too late to stop. Miraculously, the switchman managed to avert the disaster by changing over the tracks just as the train reached them. But not soon enough to save himself. The switchman was run over by the passing train and his head was chopped off when his body was pulled under the car.

Since the 1700s, a light that looks like a lantern is sometimes seen in this area. If you approach the light, it disappears. Turn around quickly and you'll see it briefly reappear behind you. According to *The Fayetteville Times* photographer Billy Fisher, who grew up in the area and saw the light many years ago, it is ". . . a ball of fire. It shoots out of the woods and then floats just over the tracks and then vanishes."

Just like the Maco and Pactolus phenomena, amateurs and scientists have studied the Vander Light. Some have suggested the light comes from street lights or car lights in Stedman (a town four miles away) or maybe from phosphorous gas (commonly called swamp gas).

"I don't know the conditions there, but it's certainly possible. There's probably a phosphorous compound, maybe phosphine, and it does react in the air and liberates heat and light. That does happen around marshes," said Halbert Carmichael, a chemistry professor at North Carolina State University, when he was interviewed by *The Fayetteville Times* about the Vander Light. Many such scientific theories have been offered, but none seem to answer the question satisfactorily. For instance, the theory that the mysterious lights are nothing more than headlights off in the distance sounds plausible except these inexplicable lights were witnessed long before the invention of the automobile!

I'm not sure the Momeyer Light has ever been investigated, but it has been witnessed by dozens of folks through the years. At one time, this lonely stretch of railroad tracks off Tressell Loop Road drew many bystanders hoping to see the mysterious light. A resident who lives near the tracks, Sissell Holland, reported that there used to be cars parked all along the road. Although there are still a few curiosity seekers, folks seem to have lost interest. Or perhaps the train engineer finally found his head!

Disbelievers like to say that people are letting their eyes play tricks on them. Just try telling that to staunch believer, William Mc-

Ilwean. "I've seen it many times. It's a whitish light, and I've seen it float over and under the trestle bridge." Could he have been mistaken about what he saw? It seems doubtful since McIlwean claims he has seen the light 27 times out of the 50 visits he has made to the area, although he admits it has been several years since his last visit.

I'm more interested in what makes us remain so morbidly and eternally intrigued with lonely stretches of railroad tracks and headless ghosts.

# SPONTANEOUS FIRES
## Bladenboro

*But the most bizarre, and certainly most frightening, was when Williamson's granddaughter's dress spontaneously caught fire while she was wearing it!*

*T*hese peculiar events happened a long time ago, but they were so phenomenal that I have to share them with you. I had heard stories of these fires for many years but never was able to learn the specifics. However, an article by gifted writer Jimmy Tomlin in *Our State* (December 2005) helped fill in the details.

There was a house on Elm Street in Bladenboro (Bladen County) that endured a string of fires, starting on January 30, 1932. A farmer named Council H. Williamson and his wife owned the residence. The first fire occurred during the late afternoon. A window shade and curtain began burning in the dining room. The fire was extinguished.

Another window shade in the dining room caught fire shortly thereafter. It, too, was extinguished. On January 31, 1932, another fire began while the family was entertaining guests. It started with some bedclothes. A stack of papers stored in a closet were the origin of the next fire that same day. Also on that same day, a pair of pants hanging in a closet caught fire.

But the most bizarre, and certainly most frightening, was when Williamson's granddaughter's dress spontaneously caught fire while she was wearing it! They managed to put the fire out and the little girl was unharmed. There were several witnesses to this event.

As you can imagine, the fires became the talk of the town. The local newspaper, *Bladen Journal*, wrote some articles about it. They even printed all the theories that had been brought forth to explain these freaky fires. One theory was that the house was charged with electricity and thereby prone to fire. However, even after the power was cut off, fires continued to occur.

A Wilmington chemist believed it was due to the rat and roach paste used at the house. They contained lard and flour and white phosphorous. It was possible that they could reach a combustible state after much time, he said. Other experts dismissed this theory.

The last fire occurred at noon on February 1, 1932. Between January 30 and February 1, twenty unexplainable fires took place in this house. By the time the last fire happened, the family had already moved out. The house was guarded and no one was allowed inside. All the partially burned items were removed and sent to the state chemist for further examination.

So what caused these fires? "There was spooks in that house," longtime Bladenboro resident Jabe Frink says (who was ten years old when the fires took place).

It may just be that simple, according to the director of ParaScience International, Larry Arnold. "It sounds like the classic poltergeist fire phenomenon, where objects other than humans spontaneously burst into open-flame combustion."

Take, for instance, the little girl and her dress. Arnold says it doesn't make sense that her dress can catch fire spontaneously without her being burned. "Whether there was some kind of psychokinetic energy or some kind of environmental factor, we just can't say. History doesn't provide us enough information."

It looks like we'll never solve this mystery. The house was torn down many years ago. The fact that gives me goose bumps is that Arnolds says this is not an isolated incident. He has studied hundreds of cases of apparent spontaneous human combustion and spontaneous combustion over the past 30 years. They were all as mysterious as the 1932 Bladenboro fires.

# THE CREEPY DOOR
Hendersonville

*Although they knew it was coming, the sharp sound of the engine's whistle and the* chug-clank, chug-clank, chug-clank *that followed as the train slid across the steel tracks almost made them jump out of their skins.*

*I*n the western part of the state, on Salola Mountain near Hendersonville, there was a house with a door that became a legend. Off the kitchen was a small room once used as the servants' quarters, and later as a pantry and storage area. The door to that room wouldn't stay closed. For that reason, this house became known as "The House of the Opening Door."

The railroad tracks were only about a mile away and freight trains made regular deliveries to Hendersonville, so every time a train came through, the shrill whistle of the engine could be heard inside the house. Every time the train roared through, the door burst open. It didn't matter if the door was blocked by furniture, latched, bolted, or nailed shut—it always flew open.

Anyone who ever lived in the house was eventually driven out by the bizarre phenomenon. John and Harriet Drew and their children were among the frightened inhabitants. They had never had much money and this was the first real home they owned. The family was excited about their new home and the future, until the first time they heard a train pass by. The train always roared through late at night so family members would lie awake in bed waiting to hear the train and what always came next. Although they knew it was coming, the sharp sound of the engine's whistle and the *chug-clank, chug-clank, chug-clank* that followed as the train slid across the steel tracks almost made them jump out of their skins. The loud creaking of the old door always followed as it swung forward on its hinges. It was just too much to take night after night.

Eventually, the strange old house sat abandoned. Many couldn't believe a locked or blocked door would open unless there was some kind of scientific reason for why and how. A group of engineers, determined to explain the mystery of the door, stayed in the house for a few days. The men concluded that the house is positioned on a hill of solid rock. Under the rock there are places of dense soil, as well as spots with less soil than they should have. When the train goes by, its weight and speed jars a particular stratum of rock. This happens to be the same stratum of rock that the house is built upon, which means that the vibrations carry to the house. Since the door was measured and found not to be completely level, the vibrations are significant enough to jar the door open. The pressure of the intense vibrations causes the door to open to relieve the pressure. This means that even if the door is locked or blocked, the pressure causes it to burst open.

With a scientific-sounding explanation to explain the door, folks felt better about the old house, and it was inhabited again. The Jones family moved in and turned the run-down house into a fine home. Late one night, some family members were gathered in the living room and the infamous door burst open. But no train had passed through, nor was there anything else that would have caused a vibration! Other former inhabitants always claimed there was more to the door than reason could explain. They say secured objects have flown out of the little storage room and across the living room and they have heard what sounds like shuffling feet coming from the small room. All told, it is easy to understand why no one dares to call "The House of the Opening Door" home.

# HOW TO CONDUCT A GHOST HUNT

*T*he second most-asked question I get is "How do you know if a place is really haunted?" (Obviously, the most popular question is "Have you seen a ghost or had a ghostly experience?")

To determine if a place is indeed haunted, an investigation must be conducted. I'll use an example to help you understand the process. The State Capitol Building in Raleigh is reportedly haunted. These claims come from many credible persons over a span of many years. A former chief of Museum and Visitor Services, Ed Morris, has been interviewed about the matter and he says that numerous visitors and staff have had some eerie encounters. "People get tapped on the shoulder a lot," says Morris.

A historian with the Capitol, Raymond Beck, once told a reporter about a disturbing evening. "It was in 1981; we were restoring the library. I was standing in the gallery. I was placing books on the shelves, and I felt the hair on the back of my neck stand on end. I felt as if somebody was standing about a foot behind me looking over my shoulder as I worked. That happened three times in one evening. After the first incident, I told the guard that if he saw people running down the stairs later in the night to be sure to hit the second one—'cause the first one would be me!"

Professional ghost hunters have been called in to find out what's going on in the capitol building. The Ghost Research Foundation of Bedford, Pennsylvania, headed by Patty Ann Wilson and Scott Crownover, were called in to investigate in 2000. Carolina Ghost Hunters, led by Anne Poole of Durham, joined them. The famed Rhine Research Center in Durham approves both organizations.

They dragged in armloads of equipment: digital cameras, 35mm cameras, small cassette machines, thermal scanners, infrared video cameras, and electromagnetic field meters.

So what did they find? They found lots of orbs. These are believed to be ghostly energy (balls of light) that cannot be seen by human eye but often turn up on developed film. They also recorded "cold spots." This is when an area suddenly gets quite cold for no apparent reason. It is popularly believed that indicates the presence of a ghost, who is "hogging" the energy, thereby creating a cold spot.

However, their best evidence of a supernatural presence was gathered a couple of years later. The Ghost Research Foundation saw a specter in Reconstruction-era clothing sitting in the third chair of the third row of the old House Chambers.

A cassette recording picked up a strange whisper that cannot be explained by investigating parties. According to an article in *Our State*, a member of Ghost Research Foundation was sitting alone in the Senate Chamber. She made a silly remark: "I know there's something up here. I sure hope it ain't no Yankee!" After several seconds of silence, a gruff male voice with a heavy Southern accent replied, "We're 'round heah." The standard procedure for thorough investigation is to use a voice analysis, which found that the woman spoke at a level of 4,000 hertz while the unknown male voice registered at 20,000 hertz. This is much higher than the normal range of human hearing.

Another investigation launched in June 2004 yielded different results. "During the early hours of June 24, several staff and invited guests felt a 'rush of air' in the third floor corridor outside the State Library and smelled the distinct and unmistakable pungent aroma of cigar smoke wafting through that passage," according to one of the participants, historian Raymond Beck. It is generally agreed that the library is the most haunted place in the Capitol.

"I don't know that I would say I'm a ghost-believer at this point, but there is some fairly compelling evidence that there is something paranormal going on here," says Beck. UNC-TV cameraman Mike Burke agrees. He participated in one of the many investigations, which included spending many hours alone in the Capitol. He went up to the second floor to ready his equipment and eat a sandwich before the rest of the group arrived. He heard a door slam and foot-

> **About our Capitol . . .**
> The State Capitol was built in 1840 and since that
> time has undergone numerous historical renova-
> tions and restorations. At one time, the executive
> branch of the government was on the first floor, the
> second floor held the legislative branch, and the
> third floor accommodated the judicial branch and
> State Library. Nowadays, the governor and his staff
> use the first floor. The library and legislative offices
> have relocated. Guided tours of this historic edifice
> are offered. Find out how our Capitol Building was
> used during the Civil War and all about its colorful
> history. For more information, call 919-807-7975.
> One E. Edenton Street, Raleigh, NC.

steps on the third floor. He never found any humans nor saw any specters, but there was no mistaking the noises. When he reviewed the footage he had shot during that time, it revealed two flecks of light moving around before disappearing.

You may want to conduct your own investigation someday of a place you believe is haunted. There certainly is plenty of incentive. The James Randi Educational Foundation, a nonprofit group based in Ft. Lauderdale, Florida, is offering $1 million to anyone who can verify psychic, supernatural, or paranormal activity under scientific conditions. Many submissions have been made, but the foundation remains unconvinced. If you set out to find solid proof to win the prize (or just to satisfy your own curiosity), here are some tips you should know and equipment you will need.

**Do some preliminary work before the actual investigation.** Check out the area in advance. Make sure you can find the place and that you will be able to gain access. You do not want to trespass on property that is roped off, fenced in, or clearly marked "No Trespassing." Find the best parking spot and look for obstacles you could trip over in the dark, such as stumps or holes. Take note of good spots to carry out the investigation.

**Bring someone with you and be prepared**. You should never go alone in case you encounter a problem, such as car trouble or getting sick or injured. However, you shouldn't bring a large group either. Too many people tend to distract from a proper investigation. Dress appropriately. Wear comfortable shoes and bring a jacket, if necessary. Don't drink alcoholic beverages before or during the study, as you need to have your wits about you. Don't talk, smoke, or wear cologne or perfume because spirits often emit sounds and scents to get attention. Since the best "psychic" hours are late at night and into the wee morning hours, make sure your vehicle has a full tank of gas and has been serviced recently. That means that the battery is good, all tires are in good shape and there is a spare in the trunk, headlights are operating properly, and antifreeze or coolant is sufficient. It's a good idea to bring along a cell phone, in case of emergency.

**Do your homework**. Before heading out to cemeteries, schools, theaters, battlefields, churches, inns, houses, former plantation homes, lighthouses, cottages, bridges, or other possible haunted sites, talk to long-time residents, former or current owners, and historians. For information on property ownership, go to the courthouse. Get permission from the owner to be on his property. It might also be a good idea to notify local authorities so they don't show up during your investigation and interfere with it.

Go to the local newspaper office and library and look for articles about the edifice or destination. Did any significant events occur there, such as a suicide, murder, or battle? Read books by local authors. If possible, verify whether the haunting is urban legend or if there have been actual sightings or corroborating events. Explore whether there are logical explanations for incidents, such as recent construction or animals (squirrels, mice, cats, etc.). Find out if the spirit is benevolent, mischievous, or downright mean and dangerous. Learn in which spot or direction you're most likely to encounter it.

**Tools of the trade**. What should you bring on such an investigation? A basic but necessary tool is a 35mm camera (and digital camera) with high-speed film, such as 400, 800 or 1600 ASA. I've been asked about infrared film but I don't recommend it because it can be very unforgiving to amateurs. It must be handled in complete darkness and kept in a cooler so that it doesn't get too warm. Since built-in flashes have an average range of twelve feet or less, a more powerful mounted flash is highly recommended. When dropping the film off for developing, indicate on the instruction box of the envelope that you want all photos developed and returned, regardless of quality. Also, make sure the batteries have plenty of life left. Bring extra batteries, even if the ones in the camera are new or almost new. Clean the lens thoroughly with a soft cloth. There are pros and cons to both types of cameras as far as taking supernatural images so use both, if possible.

A video camera is even better than a 35mm or digital camera. It should be able to record in low light. A tripod is optional. If possible, use both a still camera and video camera.

Never leave home without a flashlight, stocked with new batteries. Note that batteries run down faster in cold weather. Some professional ghost hunters recommend bringing extra batteries in case of "interference" from the spirits. It is also a good idea to bring extra flashlights. Avoid tiny flashlights, like pocketsize or pen lights. You need something that emits a bright beam.

You should take notes, possibly even make basic drawings, including as much detail as possible of what you saw and where, so a small notepad that will fit into your pocket and a couple of pens are essential. Be sure to include every bit of information, even if it seems unimportant at the time. You may later input this information into a report called a Ghost Hunt Log. This will include how many rolls of film were shot, what the film showed when developed, if any cold spots or strange sensations were felt, total time spent at site, who participated in the investigation, exactly what equipment was used, etc.

A tape recorder with a microphone and new batteries is a good tool. There are voice-activated tape recorders on the market nowadays, which are really helpful for lengthy investigations.

Some optional tools for the serious sleuth include:

A **digital or electronic thermometer or thermal scanner** used to detect cold spots. A **motion detector** used to sense movements by unseen objects or forces. There are battery-operated ones for under $20.

An **EMF detector** reads an area's electromagnetic fields. It is commonly believed that high readings are indicative of spirits. It is a good idea to take a reading when doing the initial investigation preparation at the sight. Also, take note of things that might interfere with a normal reading, such as power lines.

Some ghost hunters say a **compass** can be used instead of this costly device because it works the same way, in principle. The needle will move wildly or shake if something is interfering with a normal reading.

While talking is not encouraged on ghost hunts, it is a good idea to be able to communicate with whomever is accompanying you, especially if you are out of sight of one another. Cheap **walkie-talkies** can be purchased at most drugstores, electronics outlets, and toy stores.

All equipment should be cleaned and calibrated beforehand to ensure accurate readings. A list of proper ghost terminology can be found in *Best Ghost Tales of South Carolina*, if you're interested. Happy hunting!

*Looking for ghosts?*

According to the Society for Paranormal Investigation Research and Information (SPIRIT), there are three ways that ghosts show up in photos:

- as mist (foglike discoloration)
- as vortex (crescent-shaped pale areas that are usually white)
- as orbs (these round pale areas resembling globes or balls of light are the most common)

# RESOURCES

*Note: The following websites might be useful to those who are interested in learning more about this subject, but neither the author nor the publisher endorses them or the links they may offer.*

**The ShadowLands** is a useful website that contains many ghost stories submitted by researchers and visitors alike, as well as photos, articles, a listing of haunted places, and a training and tips page. It also has an interesting feature, "Find a Grave," which lists brief biographies and burial sites for famous people such as William Shakespeare and Marilyn Monroe. www.theshadowlands.net

For a comprehensive directory of haunted places, check out **www.haunted-places.com**

**Haunted North Carolina, Inc.**
P.O. Box 4941
Chapel Hill, NC 27515
1-866-HAUNTNC (428-6862)
www.hauntednc.com
This nonprofit organization, based in North Carolina, is "dedicated to the research and investigation of haunting and ghost phenomena, the collection of data related to these events, and sharing of information." They have been studying ghosts and hauntings since 1992.

**Rhine Research Center** in Durham, founded by Dr. J.B. Rhine. This facility is world-renowned for its work in the field of parapsychology. It used to be part of Duke University but separated from the school in the 1960s. They offer nondegree summer courses in paranormal studies. There are some foreign schools that offer degree programs in parapsychology. An excellent program is available at the University of Edinburgh. The school offers a doctorate degree in Psychology with an emphasis on Parapsychology. The Rhine Research Center is located at 402 North Buchanan Boulevard (adjoining the east campus of Duke University), Durham, NC 27701. Telephone: (919) 688-8241. www.rhine.org

**Carolina Ghost Watch Club** was founded in 2005 by author Terrance Zepke. Twice a year she shares her latest ghostly discoveries (and other relevant information on the Carolinas) with everyone who is interested in obtaining the free newsletter. She hopes to offer ghost tours in the future. For more information or to sign up, go to www.terrancezepke.com.

For more information on North Carolina destinations, contact the **North Carolina Travel and Tourism Division Department of Commerce** at 430 N. Salisbury Street, Raleigh, NC 27611. Call 800-VISITNC or (919) 733-4171, or visit www.visitnc.com.

Throughout history, almost every culture has acknowledged ghosts. The Egyptians called them khus. The Romans labeled the good spirits as lares and the bad ones as lemures. The Japanese call them shojos, while the Irish refer to them as tash. In India, there are several different classifications of ghosts, from bautas to mumiais. Some Native Americans call them spooks. At one time, Icelandic law sanctioned judicial refuge against bothersome spirits. Victims were permitted to resurrect spirits before the court to put a restraining order against offending ghosts!

# APPENDIX

This is a report filed by Coast Guard Station Surfman C.P. Brady of Coast Guard Station No. 183 on the *Carroll A. Deering*.
Courtesy of the Outer Banks History Center.

TREASURY DEPARTMENT,
U. S. COAST GUARD.
Form 2625.
F. C., May 1-16.

No. 2

## REPORT OF ASSISTANCE RENDERED

Coast Guard Station No. 183          District No. 7

Jan. 31 and Feb. 4, 19 21
(Date of casualty.)

| | |
|---|---|
| 1. Nationality, name, and rig | American schooner, Carroll A. Deering |
| 2. Hail port and gross tonnage | Bath Me. 2,114. |
| 3. Where from and where bound | Not known |
| 4. Number of days out | Not known |
| 5. Number of crew (including master) | Not known |
| 6. Number of passengers | Not known |
| 7. Estimated value of vessel | Not known |
| 8. Estimated value of cargo | No cargo |
| 9. Nature of cargo | No cargo |
| 10. Estimated damage to vessel | Total loss |
| 11. Estimated damage to cargo | No cargo |
| 12. Name and address of — Master | Not known |
| Owner | G.G. Deering Co., Bath, me. |
| 13. Supposed cause of DISASTER. | Thick weather |
| 14. Nature of—stranded, collided, etc. | Aground |
| 15. Time of day or night, and date | Discovered at 6:30 a.m. January 31, 1921 |
| 16. Exact location—direction and distance from the station | N.W. Point of S.W. Diamond shoal, 9 miles S. and Surfman Andrew Gray. |
| 17. Discovered by whom, and time of discovery | 6:30am, Jan. 31 1921 by surfman C.P. Brady |
| 18. Direction and force of wind — WEATHER. | S.W. 5. |
| 19. State of sea and tide | Rough sea, Strong tide. |

4a

20. Temperature and weather symbols................ Tem:50. M.

ASSISTANCE RENDERED.
21. Time of starting to scene................ 7:30 a.m.

22. Time of arrival at scene................ 11:30 a.m.

23. Time of launching boat................ 10:00 a.m.

24. Number of shots fired................ None

25. If any shots were unsuccessful, state briefly cause, each
    case................ None

26. What members of the crew did not participate in the
    operations, and why?................ F.M.Miller absent sick, W.R.Midgett on
    liberty, L.G.Hooper on leave, C.D.Burrus
    absent sick.

27. Number and names of persons lost................ Not known

28. Number of persons resuscitated from apparent death by
    drowning or exposure to cold................ None

29. Number of bodies found, and disposition made of same.... None

30. Number of persons sheltered at station, how long, and
    number of meals furnished................ None

31. Accidents to crew of station................ None

32. Damage to boats or apparatus................ None

33. If anything occurred to interfere with operations, state
    fully the nature and cause................ Nothing occurred

34. At what time (give date, hour, and minute) and in what
    manner was cutter notified?................ 1:30 p.m. (Via) Cape Hatteras Radio station

35. Was vessel assisted in danger of damage or loss?........ No

36. Were the lives of persons on board imperiled?............ No persons aboard.

145

# PHOTO AND ILLUSTRATION CREDITS

Photos, unless otherwise indicated, are by Terrance Zepke.

Page 12: Courtesy of North Carolina Collection, University of North Carolina at Chapel Hill

Page 33: Courtesy of the N.C. Division of Archives and History

Page 43: Courtesy of the Cape Fear Convention & Visitors Bureau

Page 53: Courtesy of Wordwright Communications.

Pages 61 and 64: Courtesy of the Grove Park Inn Resort.

Pages 76 and 77: Courtesy of Ewart M. Ball Collection, Ramsey Library Special Collections, University of North Carolina at Asheville.

Page 81: Courtesy of Davidson College Library Archives.

Page 100: Courtesy of the Outer Banks History Center.

Drawings by Julie Rabun
Pages 18, 39, 74, 79, 90, 107, 110, 114, 117, 123, 128

Drawings by Michael Swing
Pages 2, 9, 28, 58, 67, 93

Map on page 5 created by Charles House

# INDEX

If you enjoyed reading this book, here are some other books from Pineapple Press on related topics. For a complete catalog, write to Pineapple Press, P.O. Box 3889, Sarasota, FL 34230 or call 1-800-PINEAPL (746-3275). Or visit our website at www.pineapplepress.com.

*Best Ghost Tales of South Carolina.* The actors of South Carolina's past linger among the living in these thrilling collection of ghost tales. Use Zepke's tips to conduct your own ghost hunt. (pb)

*Coastal North Carolina.* Terrance Zepke visits the Outer Banks and the Upper and Lower Coasts to bring you the history and heritage of coastal communities, main sites and attractions, sports and outdoor activities, lore and traditions, and even fun ways to test your knowledge of this unique region. Over 50 photos. (pb)

*Coastal South Carolina.* From Myrtle Beach to Beaufort, South Carolina's Lowcountry is steeped in history and full of charm, and author Terrance Zepke makes sure you don't miss any of it. A must-have for vacationers, day-trippers, armchair travelers, and people looking to relocate to the area. (pb)

*Ghosts of the Carolina Coasts.* Taken from real-life occurrences and Carolina Lowcountry lore, these thirty-two spine-tingling ghost stories take place in prominent historic structures of the region. (pb)

*Ghosts and Legends of the Carolina Coasts.* More spine-chilling tales and fascinating legends from the coastal regions of North and South Carolina. (pb)

*Lighthouses of the Carolinas.* Eighteen lighthouses aid mariners traveling the coasts of North and South Carolina. Here is the story of each, from origin to current status, along with visiting information and photographs. Newly revised to include up-to-date information on the long-awaited and much-debated Cape Hatteras Lighthouse move, plus websites for area visitors' centers and tourist bureaus. Over 100 photos. (pb)

*Pirates of the Carolinas, 2nd Ed.* Thirteen of the most fascinating buccaneers in the history of piracy, including Henry Avery, Blackbeard, Anne Bonny, Captain Kidd, Calico Jack, and Stede Bonnet. (pb)